Two fancy varieties of rabbits sharing some green...

RABBITS

COMPLETELY ILLUSTRATED IN FULL COLOR

A Himalayan marked Netherland Dwarf rabbit. Photo by Michael Gilroy.

Marshal Merton

Distributed in the UNITED STATES by T.F.H. Publications, Inc., 211 West Sylvania Avenue, Neptune City, NJ 07753; in CANADA to the Pet Trade by H & L Pet Supplies Inc., 27 Kingston Crescent, Kitchener, Ontario N2B 2T6; Rolf C. Hagen Ltd., 3225 Sartelon Street, Montreal 382 Quebec; in CANADA to the Book Trade by Macmillan of Canada (A Division of Canada Publishing Corporation), 164 Commander Boulevard, Agincourt, Ontario M1S 3C7; in ENGLAND by T.F.H. Publications Limited, 4 Kier Park, Ascot, Berkshire SL5 7DS; in AUSTRALIA AND THE SOUTH PACIFIC by T.F.H. (Australia) Pty. Ltd., Box 149, Brookvale 2100 N.S.W., Australia; in NEW ZEALAND by Ross Haines & Son, Ltd., 18 Monmouth Street, Grey Lynn, Auckland 2 New Zealand; in SINGAPORE AND MALAYSIA by MPH Distributors (S) Pte., Ltd., 601 Sims Drive, #03/07/21, Singapore 1438; in the PHILIPPINES by Bio-Research, 5 Lippay Street, San Lorenzo Village, Makati Rizal; in SOUTH AFRICA by Multipet Pty. Ltd., 30 Turners Avenue, Durban 4001. Published by T.F.H. Publications Inc. Manufactured in the United States of America . by T.F.H. Publications, Inc.

Introduction

The origin of the domestic rabbit is steeped in history, but there is no doubt that it is the descendant of the common wild European rabbit, said to have originated on the Iberian Peninsula where the first domestic forms also probably arose. It was already well-known during the time of the Roman Empire, and it was probably the Roman legions which were largely responsible for the spread of the rabbit throughout Europe at this time in history. Both domestic and wild rabbits seemed to make their appearance in certain areas at roughly the same periods and there is evidence to suggest that wild rabbits existing in many areas of Northern Europe today are descendants of domestic rabbits which escaped, or were released by early rabbit keepers. After a few generations in the wild, even fancy rabbits soon assume the average size and the gray/brown coloration of their wild cousins. For centuries, the domestic rabbit has been kept mainly for meat, sometimes for fur or 'wool' and, last but certainly not least, as a pet or exhibition animal. Initially, the rabbits were kept in a fenced off area of land known as a warren and the animals were allowed to burrow and breed as they wished, being collected for food at regular intervals - a convenient and inexpensive contribution to the economy. Such warrens were well established in Britain and other Northern European countries by the Middle Ages but the earliest known references to the animal in the British Isles occurred during the 12th Century. There is no Anglo-Saxon or Celtic word for the rabbit, and they were first described as 'coneys'; taken from the Latin *cuniculus*. The term 'rabbit' came later and initially described the young of the animal. In *The Noble Art of Venerie or Hunting* (1575) it states that 'the conie beareth hyr rabettes XXX dayes, and then kindeleth'. It was not until the 18th Century that the term "rabbit" became universally accepted as the English word for the animal. Other European languages have opted to retain the Latin root thus: *konijn* (Dutch), *Kaninchen* (German), *coniglio* (Italian), *conejo* (Spanish), *kanin* (Swedish), but *lapin* (French).

The rabbit is one of many species in the mammalian order Lagomorpha, which also includes the hares and the pikas, most of which have large, prominent ears, strong hind limbs and a streamlined body built for speed, the

Shown is a Smoke Pearl Netherland Dwarf rabbit, a fancy variety developed for exhibition and the pet trade. Photo by Michael Gilroy.

prime purpose of which is to escape from their numerous carnivorous enemies including man himself. They share with the rodents the unique, evergrowing, chisel-like incisor teeth which require almost constant use to prevent excessive growth. The wild rabbit, *Oryctolagus cuniculus,* has colonized every continent, helped by accidental or deliberate introduction by man and, as is so often the case when nature is interfered with, has become a serious pest in many areas. Rabbits are responsible for considerable damage to agricultural and garden crops, turning their attentions to the gnawing of tree bark in the winter.

9

Various methods of rabbit control, ranging from shooting to ferreting, netting to gassing have never been a serious threat to prolific rabbit populations. In desperation, the virus *Myxomatosis cuniculus*, first discovered in Uruguay in 1896, was developed in France by Dr. Armand Delille and inoculated into a pair of rabbits which were later released into the wild. Nobody could have envisaged the rapidity with which this dreadful disease could spread, and within one year of its introduction in 1952 it had advanced on all fronts into most areas of Western Europe. Within three years, an astounding 99 percent of the wild rabbit population had been destroyed, partially helped by man transporting sick rabbits from area to area. The disease itself is transmitted from animal to animal by the rabbit flea, *Spilopsyllus cuniculi* or by the mosquito.

The disease has since been introduced into other continents and has proven to be an effective control against wild rabbit populations, which now never reach the vast numbers existing in the early part of the century. However, the hardy and ubiquitous rabbit has never been completely wiped out by the virus; in some areas indeed, it seems to have developed an immunity to it.

The domestic rabbit has been of great economic importance to many peoples, and during times of national emergencies when meat becomes scarce, there has usually been an increase in rabbit production for food. This was partially noticeable in Europe in the periods during and immediately following the two World Wars when numerous people relied on rabbit meat as their major or even sole source of animal protein. Breeds such as the New Zealand and the Flemish Giant were specially developed for meat production. The rabbit's coat has also not been neglected and, even today, 'coney fur' is an accepted material in the world of fashion. Certain long-haired breeds such as the Angora produce reasonable quantities of 'wool' which can be sheared at regular intervals. An advantage of keeping 'wool' producing rabbits, of course, is that the animal does not require to be slaughtered in order to gain the product, and the product may be obtained time and time again.

It was during the Middle Ages that keeping rabbits in hutches first developed, though not on the scale it is known today. Monasteries were known to have their rabbit studs, whence they soon spread to the peasant population. Early domestic rabbits were probably similar in all respects to the wild variety, but it was not long before color mutations appeared, which is usually the case with any animals which are extensively bred in captivity. By exploiting these mutations, early 'geneticists' were able to begin to develop the forerunners of all the well-known breeds of fancy and utility rabbits known today. Modern rabbit breeding and the diversification of particular varieties came into its own in the mid-19th Century, although the emphasis would have been on rapidity of growth and size, rather than on the development of fancy breeds. New breeds of rabbit were produced and recognized from many parts of Europe. The rabbit popularity explosion soon spread to other parts of the world, including the U.S.A., Asia and Australasia and it can now be said that the keeping of rabbits is a hobby or pastime of relative popularity in all corners of the globe.

The development of most fancy varieties took its momentum at the beginning of the present century and new forms are being produced even today. The interest in rabbit keeping surely evolved from the fact that the animals could be kept in relatively small spaces, they were inexpensive to feed, came in a variety of colors and sizes and, last but not least, they made docile and endearing pets which could be safely handled, even by small children. Rabbits are not necessarily just childrens' pets however and it is probable that the majority of serious rabbit fanciers are adults from all walks of life. Many such fanciers are members of rabbit clubs, where ideas can be exchanged, stock can be discussed and regular exhibitions held to keep the standard of breeds at their best. Many fanatical fanciers began their 'careers' in rabbit keeping by having a single rabbit pet as a child, this increasing to a pair and eventually to a stud as the enthusiasm developed.

This small volume is intended to introduce the beginner to the delights of rabbit keeping. Whether it is intended to keep a single animal as a pet or a number of animals in stud, the author has attempted to deal with all aspects of the care and breeding of these charming animals in a clear and concise manner. It is hoped that the following text will guide the prospective rabbit enthusiast into a pastime which will give him countless hours of lasting pleasure.

Accommodations

One of the first questions to be asked when one decides to keep a rabbit, or indeed any other kind of pet animal, is: "Where am I going to keep it, and what am I going to keep it in?" This question has to be asked, and the answer carefully considered before one takes the plunge and obtains an animal. Unfortunately, far too many pets are acquired before due consideration has been given to the problems involved and this often ends in disaster, usually for the animal!

Ideally, one who keeps rabbits should also have a garden at least, so that the animals can be given a certain amount of free exercise in the fresh air. That said, however, the rabbit's normal accommodation should take up little more room than a large television set or a bar. Single pet rabbits are normally kept in little cages called hutches and these may be kept indoors or out, although the latter will obviously require considerably more sophisticated construction for protection from the weather. Although rabbits are generally considered to be gregarious animals, it is always best to keep them singly in the small areas available in hutches, thus avoiding any unnecessary injury which may arise through squabbling. The exceptions to this rule are when pairs are introduced for mating, when mothers are rearing their litters and when groups are kept in outdoor pens.

Above: *The dimensions of a hutch should depend on the size of the rabbit you intend to keep.*

Indoor Hutches

Indoor hutches are those which are kept either in the owner's living accommodations, or in a garage, outside structure, or shed. Providing such an area is frost-free and reasonably draft-proof, there is no need for the elaborate construction required for outdoor hutches. The hutch is really little more than a wooden box, open at the front and

divided into a larger and a smaller compartment, the former for exercise, the latter for sleeping quarters. The size will of course vary depending on the breed of rabbit to be kept but for a medium-sized breed such as an English, or Dutch, a

hutch some 100 cm (39 in) long, by 40 cm (16 in) deep, by 40 cm (16 in) high, should be adequate. The sleeping compartment should take up about one third of the length and the dividing panel should have an entrance hole of a size through which the rabbit can com

Two doors are affixed to the front of the hutch, a solid one for access to the sleeping quarters and a larger, wire mesh covered door for the exercise and viewing area. Although slightly more expensive, galvanized weld mesh, with a gauge of about 15 mm (1/2 in), is more attractive, stronger and easier to fix than the rather flimsy, so-called chicken wire. The mesh should be attached to the inside of the frame with galvanized staples in such a way that the wire covers most of the timber, thus making it difficult for the inmates to gnaw at the frame.

If the hutch is kept indoors in warm surroundings, the sleeping compartment can be dispensed with and the frame door can cover the whole of the front. In such cases, a sleeping box can be provided. This can be of 5 mm (1/4 in) ply with a 30 cm (12 in) square base,

Indoor Hutches

Arrangement of hutches for display of show rabbits in England. Photo by Michael Gilroy.

three sides of 15 cm (6 in) height and a fourth side as

an entrance, just 5 cm (2 in) high. The top remains open and the bedding material is placed loosely in the box.

Good quality hutches can be purchased from your pet suppliers at reasonable prices, or it is quite often possible to get a good, second-hand hutch through an ad in your local paper. The do-it-yourself expert can soon construct a hutch to his own design.

Below: A layer of bedding material protects the hocks from injury, it should be changed often for sanitary reasons. Photo by Vince Serbin.

It can be made of 10 mm (1/2 in) ply, or preferably, tongued and grooved boarding, which is much more attractive and durable. Be sure that no projecting edges of timber are left on the inside of the hutch, where the animals may obtain a purchase with their gnawing incisors, which could result in a large hole in the hutch wall and effect an escape!

The floor of the hutch should preferably be of solid plywood and an optional extra would be a removable sliding tray to cover the whole floor area, thus simplifying the routine cleaning chores. The position of the hinges and the catches of the doors is of little importance, providing they facilitate easy, obstruction-free access to the hutch interior at feeding or cleaning time.

The interior of the hutch should be painted with primer, undercoat and a good grade of lead-free topcoat, which should be thoroughly dry before the animals are installed. A coating of gloss paint on the interior walls will make it much easier to keep them clean. Alternatively, two or three coats of exterior quality varnish can be used to seal the surface of the wood. The outside of the hutch can either be left as bare wood, painted or, most attractively, stained and varnished.

Indoor hutches kept in outdoor structures should

Above: *You can not expect to keep a large rabbit breed in this hutch intended to house Netherland Dwarf rabbits.*

be placed in areas which are well lit, adequately ventilated but out of direct drafts. The advantages of indoor hutches are manifold; they need not be

15

as substantial as their outdoor counterparts and are therefore cheaper to construct, and animals will be safer from inclement weather, particularly in those areas where the

Below: *An outdoor hutch must adequately protect a rabbit from the elements. Photo by Mervin F. Roberts.*

climate is unreliable. Moreover, the rabbit keeper himself will find it much more pleasant to service his hutches indoors when the outside weather is bad.

Outdoor Hutches

A single outdoor hutch is basically the same as an indoor one, except that it should be of sturdier construction and weatherproof. Rabbits are hardy animals and providing they are kept in dry, draft-proof quarters and receive a balanced diet, there is really no reason why they cannot be kept in outside hutches, even in the most unsavory winters. Outdoor hutches must, of course have a sloping roof to allow rain to run off. To protect the walls, the edges of the roof should overlap them at least by 5 cm (2 in) on all sides. The roof can be made from a solid sheet of plywood with a slope to the back of the hutch of not less than 30°. The roof must be covered with roofing felt which can be battened down with strips of 1 cm x 2 cm (1/2 in x 1 in) timber running from front to back at intervals of about 20 cm (8 in). For added proofing, the roofing felt can extend right down the back of the cage and a sheet of heavy gauge polyethylene can be attached to the front of the roof with a batten. A further batten is attached to the bottom edge of the sheet and this can be

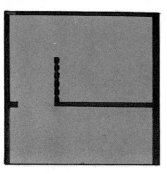

allowed to hang down the front of the hutch during bad weather and at night time. During the day, in fine weather the polyethylene is simply rolled up around the batten and installed in a pair of brackets which can be affixed to the ends of the roof.

All outside hutches should be fixed to a sturdy base and be at least 45 cm

This hutch has been situated in a fence-enclosed area to keep other animals away from the rabbits; note that the roof slopes to allow rain runoff. The hutch has been constructed of plywood, and of course only plywood that is suitable for use outdoors went into its constructions. The inset shows the floor plan of the hutch's interior.

(18 in) from the floor, as narrow spaces left between the floor of the hutch and the ground

17

would soon be colonized by rodents, or other undesirable pests, which could spread disease to your stock and steal the food. The exposed timbers of the base and the outside of the hutch should be treated with a wood preservative and allowed to dry out thoroughly before any animals are introduced. Hutches may be built in tiers of up to three high; any higher will make cleaning awkward. A maximum sized unit should consist of no more than nine hutches, in three tiers of three rows; a greater number would make the unit almost impossible to move, should this become necessary.

Outside hutches should be placed in a fairly sheltered area, preferably backing onto the wall of a building and facing in a direction that will allow sunlight to enter the hutches for at least a few hours each day; even rabbits can be fond of sunbathing and there is evidence to suggest that they derive some benefit from it. At the same time, however, in hot climates and in particularly warm summers, care should be taken to ensure that the hutches do not become overheated and in some cases, it may be necessary to erect some kind of shading.

Above: *Soiled bedding should be discarded properly to prevent the possible spread of vermin or disease. Photo by Vince Serbin.*

Breeding Hutches

Breeding hutches, whether indoor or outdoor, are the same basic pattern as the single rabbit hutch, but perhaps with the sleeping compartment a little larger to accommodate the mother and growing litter. In addition, a board about

10 cm (4 in) wide, should be fitted along the floor, just inside the inspection

door, to prevent youngsters from falling out when the door is opened. Another recommendation, of benefit to the doe, so that she may occasionally escape the ravaging attentions of the feeding litter, is the installation of a shelf above the nest area. Such a shelf should be about 20 cm (8 in) from the floor and, for a medium sized doe, about 15 cm (6 in) wide. She can then jump up on to the shelf when she needs a rest from suckling.

Bedding
The most convenient type of floor litter for the whole of the hutch floor is a substantial covering of clean sawdust or woodshavings. Such a material is absorbent and will take up the rabbits' urine. An additional advantage is the insulating properties to the hutch floor, especially in those kept outdoors. Quantities of sawdust or shavings can usually be obtained very cheaply, or even free, from a lumber merchant, who is sometimes only too glad to get rid of it. Care should be taken to ensure that such materials are from clean, untreated timber as many wood preservatives could have a detrimental effect on the health of the animals. The dry shavings or sawdust can be collected and stored in large plastic bags until required for use.

Nesting material will usually take the form of hay or straw; the former will be eaten by the rabbits as well as used to build a nest. Straw is often chewed up into narrow strands to make softer nesting material. The sleeping quarters should be inspected regularly and bedding material replenished as necessary; a loose bundle pushed into the quarters will soon be formed into a cozy nest by the rabbit.

triangular in shape and can be of any size, but obviously needs to be light enough to be moved about. The wire mesh covered frame is constructed from timber and about one quarter of

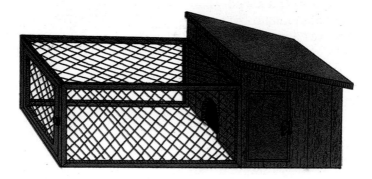

This Morant pen is slightly different from the original design by Major G. Morant, but it serves the same purpose. Illustration by Scott Boldt.

Morant Pens

A convenient method of allowing small groups of rabbits to enjoy the fresh air and to obtain some natural food is to house them in portable pens which can be moved around on grassy areas. Such a pen is often known as a Morant, named after a Major G. Morant, who is said to have pioneered this method towards the end of the last century. A Morant hutch is essentially

its length is taken up by a weatherproof shelter. The floor of the shelter is raised slightly so that the rabbits have a dry area to retire to should they so wish. The bottom of the pen is wired with a large gauge mesh of about 5 cm (2 in) which will prevent the animals from burrowing out but will still allow them to graze. Similar types of pen may be of square or rectangular shape, the essential point being that the rabbits can benefit from the natural food. Such pens are usually fixed with handles, to facilitate transport by two or more people. To avoid excessive pollution from droppings, and overgrazing, the hutches should be moved to new pasture at regular intervals. The soiled portions of land will soon recover and can be used

Water is dispensed conveniently using a water bottle. Illustration by John R. Quinn.

again, as soon as a fresh crop of grass has appeared. In spite of the value of natural feeding in this manner, the rabbits should still receive their regular rations of dry food. Such pens are particularly useful for the rearing of freshly weaned litters during the warmer months of the year.

Colony Pens

Some people like to keep rabbits in a kind of colony system, usually running several does with a single buck in a fixed pen, similar to a chicken run. If more than one buck is to be kept, it is essential that an adequate area is provided, otherwise fighting for territorial space is likely to

A strong fence prevents escapes and provides protection against dogs, cats, and wild animals.

ensue. Such colony pens can be made to look quite attractive and can be planted with one or two flowering shrubs (non-poisonous), the stems protected from the rabbits by wire sleeves. To prevent the rabbits from burrowing out of the pen, the wire mesh should extend into the ground about 15 cm (6 in) and bend inwards at right angles for a further 30 cm (12 in). As rabbits invariably start to burrow near the edge of the enclosure, the wire will effectively prevent them from making an escape. The shelter can be of timber or brickwork, with a removable roof to facilitate cleaning. The floor of the shelter is best raised at least 15 cm (6 in) from the ground to avoid dampness and the rabbits can gain access to the bolthole by ascending a wooden ramp. The imaginative rabbit keeper can come up with all sorts of interesting designs for housing his rabbits and the shelters (which should have several compartments) can be made to look like miniature Alpine villas, Chinese pagodas or anything else which tickles the fancy.

In particularly wet areas, colony pens may become oversaturated with water and unpleasant mud will ensue. One method of surmounting this problem is by digging out the base of the enclosure to a depth of about 30 cm (12 in) and filling it with 25 cm (10 in) of well rammed stone or brick rubble. The remaining 5 cm (2 in) is filled with coarse sand, which can be changed and raked at regular intervals as it becomes soiled. Areas of the sand can regularly be covered with fresh turf to provide grass for the rabbits. In some cases the floors of colony pens may be concreted or slabbed, ensuring that there is a slope and a drain to take away water in wet weather. An advantage of such a solid floor is that it can be thoroughly scrubbed and hosed down at regular intervals.

Design of a breeding hutch with several compartments. Three cages, above one another, reach a height of 2 m. Each compartment is equipped with a hay rack, also.

Nutrition

All animals require a balanced diet in order to maintain the best of physical health and to ensure that all bodily functions are satisfactorily performed. Wild animals obtain their balanced diets

Keep your pet rabbit away from any strange plant. It may be poisonous, thorny or cause allergies.

in various ways; there are meat-eaters called carnivores, vegetable eaters called herbivores and those which eat some of each, called omnivores. Each animal has a special digestive system equipped to deal with the types of food forming the staple diet in the area to which the animal is native.

Rabbits are herbivores and, in the wild, live on various grasses, seeds, green foliage, roots and bark, from which their digestive systems extract the necessary quantities of nutrients. All balanced diets should contain proteins, carbohydrates, fats, vitamins and minerals in varying quantities, depending on times of the year, activity rhythms, breeding cycles and other such things. The functions of these various nutrients are as follows:

Proteins: Probably the most important single item in the diet, proteins are necessary for the growth, repair and replacement of body tissues, ranging from muscle to inner organs such as heart, kidneys, liver and the brain. There are two main classes of protein, animal and vegetable, the former being available to meat eaters in its meat form. Herbivores, however, have to convert second class vegetable protein to animal protein by special digestive processes. The main sources of proteins in the rabbit's diet are seed and grain, with smaller amounts in green food and hay.

Carbohydrates: These include the starches and

Coltsfoot

Shepherds Purse

Yarrow

Dandelion.

Clover

SOME EDIBLE GREEN FOODS.

the sugars which are burned up in the muscles to provide energy and body warmth. Without them, animals would be unable to retain the body temperatures which are so important to them in cold weather. Carbohydrates are found in most kinds of

Above are shown drawings of some of the edible green foods that grow wild; avoid sprayed vegetation.

food in varying quantities, but are particularly abundant in cereals and root vegetables.

Fats: In rabbits, these are derived from vegetable

oils and are also manufactured in the body from excess carbohydrates. Fat is deposited as adipose tissue subcutaneously and acts as an insulant and as a shock absorber. During times of hardship, fat can be reconverted to carbohydrate for energy and warmth.

Vitamins: There are a number of vitamins which are important to the health of rabbits and fortunately, most of them are available in common food items. Vitamin A, which is contained in green and root vegetables is used by the body in the assimilation of food, general metabolism and the correct functioning of lymph and other glands. Vitamin B_1, sometimes known as thiamine, is found in cereals and is important in the synthesis of carbohydrates in the body. Vitamin B_2, found in cereals and grasses, performs a similar function with proteins. Several other vitamins in the B complex perform varying functions in the body. Vitamin C is commonly found in greenfoods, root vegetables and fruits and is necessary for the performance of various bodily functions. A lack of

this vitamin in man causes scurvy. Vitamin D which is found in oils, is important to the assimilation of the minerals calcium and phosphorus. Vitamin E, found in seeds and grain, is sometimes known as the fertility vitamin and is important to breeding animals.

Minerals: The salts of various elements are a necessary part of the diet and compounds of such items as copper, iodine, iron, magnesium, potassium, sulphur, phosphorus and calcium are important in minute quantities. Most of these elements are found in common foodstuffs, although it may be found that certain areas are deficient in one or more of them. The most important minerals are calcium and phosphorus which, with the assistance of Vitamin D, build up the bony skeleton. The absence of any of these three items in growing youngsters will

Above: *Arrangement of pens in a commercial rabbitry.*

result in rickets.

Water: Considering that water forms more than 90 percent of a living body, it is amazing how often it is left out of a list of essential nutrients. Without water, all of the other nutrients would be useless as it is the water which dissolves and transports them around the body. Since it is already contained in the fresh vegetable food given to rabbits, they will not necessarily drink a great deal of extra water. However, fresh water should be available at all times, either in a heavy earthenware, or non-tip plastic dish, or preferably in a water bottle which can be suspended upside down outside the hutch, with a drinking spout passing through the wire mesh. Rabbits which are fed a diet predominantly of pellets or other dry food will drink much more water than those given regular fresh vegetable food.

In order to ensure that your rabbit gets a balanced diet, it should be given as wide a range of dry and fresh foods as possible, or alternatively, supplied with the special pellet foods available from pet stores. Such pellets are manufactured from ground hay, straw, grain, seed, fishmeal and other such ingredients, fortified with minerals and vitamins and then compressed into conveniently sized pellets designed to provide a rabbit with a complete diet. Theoretically, these rabbit pellets, plus water, are all an animal requires to keep it in the best of health, and many commercial breeders and laboratories give their rabbits little else. The average rabbit fancier,

Food hoppers prevent overfeeding, because measured amounts can be provided at regular intervals. Photo by Vince Serbin.

however, will feel that a monotonous diet of pellets would be a bore for their pets and use them only as part of a more varied diet.

Dry Foods
Dry foods should be given to the rabbits in earthenware dishes, which are usually available from pet suppliers. Such dishes are hygienic as they are easy to clean, and their weight prevents them from being tipped over by the animals. Plastic dishes are not so convenient as not only will they be soon tipped over by the animals, but regular cleaning will result in scratching and fraying of the surface, resulting in a breeding ground for potentially dangerous bacteria.

Fresh Foods
Under this category we can include greens, root vegetables and fruits. Rabbits should receive some of these daily, sparingly, as a supplement to the dried food which is the staple diet. Even when there is a surfeit of certain vegetables, which may happen at certain times of the year, the rabbit keeper should refrain from giving his animals excessive quantities, which could result in unpleasant stomach upsets. Rabbits will eat almost every vegetable which we also eat and the kitchen can be a source of valuable offcuts which should be washed and shaken dry before feeding them to the rabbits. Greenfoods such

as cabbage, spinach, lettuce, cauliflower, celery, and leeks will be taken eagerly. Root vegetables diet. As an occasional treat, rabbits can be given small quantities of such fruits as apples, pears or

Foxglove

Lily of the Valley

Convolvulus

Deadly Nightshade.

Buttercup

SOME POISONOUS PLANTS.

such as carrots (particularly), turnips, swedes, kohlrabi, parsnips and even beetroot are a valuable addition to the melons.

The countryside is a veritable gold mine of fresh green food in the summer months and it should not be beyond the realm of possibility to go throughout the season without having to buy a single amount of this material. Many garden weeds are excellent rabbit foods and include such items as chickweed, dandelion, clover, dead spread disease to your stock. Also, it is advisable to gather it well away from public highways, thus avoiding any which is polluted with exhaust fumes or insecticides. There are many other kinds of wild foods which are suitable for rabbits and

Above: *Carrot is a good source of Vitamin A. It also stays fresh longer than other fresh plant food.*

nettle, hogweed, goosegrass, groundsel, shepherds purse, plantains, hedge parsley, sow thistle and, of course, the many kinds of seeding grasses. When collecting wild green food, be sure that it has not been polluted by dogs or other animals which could it is impossible to list them all here. In order to find out what wild foods are safe and healthy for your stock, it may be advantageous to consult other breeders (not necessarily of rabbits) of livestock in your area, who will usually be only too glad to help; there is always a certain *esprit de corps* among livestock breeders of all kinds.

A cautionary measure to be taken when collecting

wild food is to ascertain that no poisonous plants are accidentally introduced to the animals. It will pay to purchase the Encyclopedia of Pet Rabbits, published by T.F.H. Publications, in which is described poisonous plants, so that you will know which to avoid. In any case, if one is unsure about a particular plant, it should be left well alone.

Hay

Hay is treated as a separate subject here as it is important for rabbits to have it available at all times. Good quality meadow hay is fairly nutritious, can be used as bedding and the rabbits will have something to nibble at between meals. The most important function of hay in the diet however is to provide roughage. A big proportion of it consists of fibre, which is essential for the satisfactory functioning of the digestive system. There are several kinds of hay, meadow hay being a mixture of grasses and weeds. Clover hay, containing a high proportion of clover or alfalfa, is quite nutritious and enjoyed by the rabbits. Surprisingly, nettle hay is probably the most

nutritious kind and is eaten eagerly by rabbits, although they will not eat the fresh plant. If it can be obtained, nettle hay is ideal for young stock and will produce good results of growth and condition. Good quality hay should always have a sweet, pleasant smell and any which has a musty odor should be discarded, as should any with obvious signs of mold or mildew which will result if the material is baled and stored before it has thoroughly dried out. A bunch of hay can be supplied daily to rabbits in

Below: If you do not use hay as bedding, see to it that you give your rabbit a daily ration of hay for nibbling. Photo by Michael Gilroy.

their hutches. For colony pens, it is best to supply feed hay in a rack, made from wide mesh, so that the rabbits can pull out a

wastage from trampling and soiling.

Methods of Feeding

The questions of 'how

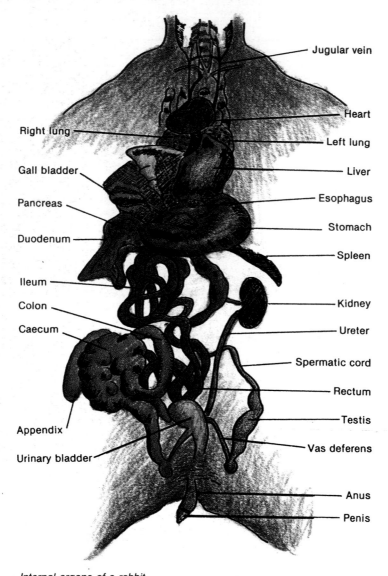

Jugular vein

Heart

Right lung

Left lung

Gall bladder

Liver

Pancreas

Esophagus

Stomach

Duodenum

Spleen

Ileum

Colon

Kidney

Caecum

Ureter

Spermatic cord

Rectum

Testis

Appendix

Vas deferens

Urinary bladder

Anus

Penis

Internal organs of a rabbit.

little at a time as they require it, thus avoiding

often?' and 'how much?' are sure to arise when one is planning a feeding system. Rabbits may feed once, twice or even three times a day, and the amounts will vary, depending on how often they are fed. Unless automatic feed hoppers are used for dry foods, it is uneconomical to feed rabbits with more than they consume in an hour or so as the food will be dragged about, trampled and wasted. Feeding twice a day is probably the best compromise to save time and to avoid wastage. Being creatures of habit, rabbits will appreciate being fed at the same times each day and will soon learn these times, waiting expectantly at the wire each time food is brought.

The Rabbit's Digestive System

The nutritional requirements of the rabbit can be perhaps better understood if one has a working knowledge of the animal's digestive system, which is somewhat different from ours. Rabbits have what, when first seen, may appear to be an unpleasant habit of eating their own droppings, but there is a logical reason for this, as will be seen later.

It can be said that the first part of digestion occurs as soon as an item of food is taken into the mouth. Rabbits have two pairs of incisors in the upper jaw, one pair in the lower. The upper pairs consist of the main, chisel-like pair at the front of the jaw, with a secondary, smaller incisor just behind

In the wild, rabbits search for edible roots as part of the diet.

and on either side of these, forming a V shaped groove, into which the pair of incisors of the lower jaw will fit. This combination forms a highly efficient shearing mechanism for cutting off pieces from items of food too large to be taken directly into the mouth. As soon as a reasonable mouthful has been assembled the grinding teeth come into action. These consist of three premolars and three molars on either side of

Food taken into the mouth is coarsely ground up by the premolars and molars which are equipped with special ridges and grinding

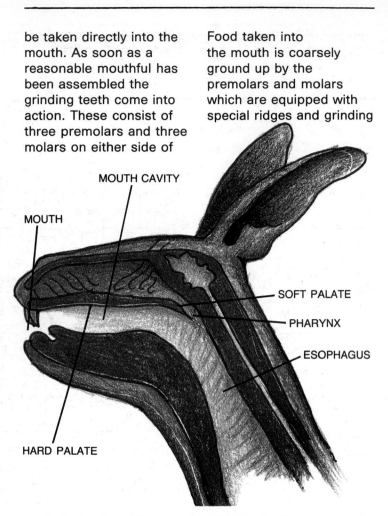

MOUTH CAVITY

MOUTH

SOFT PALATE

PHARYNX

ESOPHAGUS

HARD PALATE

Longitudinal section of the head of a rabbit showing the upper digestive tract.

the upper jaw and two premolars and three molars on either side of the lower jaw. The dental formula is expressed thus:

$$\frac{2\text{-}0\text{-}3\text{-}3}{1\text{-}0\text{-}2\ \ 3}$$

There are no canine teeth.

edges. All of a rabbit's teeth grow continually throughout its life, so it is important that the animal has something to chew on at all times. Hay should normally be available and some breeders like to provide their rabbits with twigs or small branches so that the animals have something to gnaw and also gain some nutritional benefit from the bark. Care should be taken when selecting such twigs, and poisonous varieties must be avoided.

As the food is being chewed in the mouth, saliva is released from a number of glands in the mucous membranes, not only providing lubrication for the smooth passage of the food, but also the first enzyme, which begins to convert the starches into soluble sugars. The masticated food is swallowed, and it passes through the narrow esophagus into the first part of the stomach, a storage area where further digestive juices and enzymes are added to the mixture. The posterior end of the stomach is a muscular sac, called the pylorus and it is from here that the food is forced into the first part of the small intestine, the duodenum, where it receives further enzymes and bile from the liver. It is the bile which has a major action on fats, breaking them up into minute globules which can be further acted upon by the enzymes, producing fatty acids and glycerides. The digestible food is absorbed in the lower part

of the small intestine and transmitted into the bloodstream where the various constituents are transported around the

Below: *A fancy type rabbit, like this Chocolate Tan, is best kept by itself. Photo by Vince Serbin.*

body and used as already described. The undigested food and the indigestible fibres pass into a unique portion of the rabbit's digestive system known as the caecum, where a number of bacteria species further digest the material. Having already passed the area of absorption however, the only way this material can be utilized is by swallowing it a second time.

By a process known as coprophagy, the rabbit eats the fecal pellets resulting from contractions of the caecum, directly from the anus. These are a special type of pellet, and differ from the normal, pea sized droppings which the animal discards during routine defecation. The coprophagous pellets pass through the system again, allowing the material which was bacterially digested in the caecum to be absorbed. The indigestible fibre then by-passes the caecum straight into the colon, where fluid is removed and the dryish pellets formed which pass through the rectum to be deposited as waste material. So, as can be seen, the apparently unpleasant habit of eating its own droppings is a perfectly normal part of the rabbit's physiology and allows it to gain nutrients from parts of the food which would be wasted in other animals. Additionally, there is evidence to suggest that quantities of B complex vitamins are manufactured during the secondary digestive process in the caecum, thus providing the animal with further nutrients.

Below: *The Netherland Dwarf rabbit breed is quite popular as a show rabbit and pet. Photo by Ray Hanson.*

Above: *Always choose a well-made water bottle. The spout is of heavy metal, not plastic or rubber. Photo by Vince Serbin.*

The majority of rabbit enthusiasts probably first gained their initial interest in the hobby by keeping a single pet rabbit which may have been given to them by a parent, friend or relative, often as a birthday or Christmas present. Pet rabbits as such, are often of no particular breed and indeed, may be a mixture of several. The owners of a pair of pet rabbits often have unwanted young to give away, and it is this kind of rabbit which usually fires the enthusiasm of the future exhibition breeder. There is certainly nothing wrong with keeping the single pet rabbit, whatever breed or variety it may be and indeed, it is better to gain experience with a pet rabbit first, than to practice on expensive, potential exhibition stock.

Selection

Having decided on the type of rabbit required, (and such a decision will depend on personal taste as well as on the amount of space available), and having made advance arrangements for the accommodation of the animal, steps are then taken to obtain one. Rabbits are often seen advertised in the local paper, sometimes 'free to good homes' and if one is not particular about the variety, this is an ideal way to get one's first pet. Perhaps one will elect to purchase a rabbit from a pet shop, or from a local breeder of particular varieties. Wherever rabbits are purchased, the following guidelines, which apply to all breeds, should be observed so that unhealthy stock is avoided.

The first impressions of the premises from which one hopes to obtain stock will often give one an idea of what the animals are going to be like. Untidy and inefficiently run establishments are more likely to have unhealthy rabbits than those which are sparkling with cleanliness. It does not require a practiced eye to see when hutches have been hurriedly cleaned for the benefit of the prospective purchaser and it is usually best to avoid the temptation of purchasing stock from such places. It is important to ensure that a newly purchased rabbit is in prime condition; it can be very demoralizing if one's first pet rabbit turns out to be diseased; moreover it is best to avoid the possibility of infecting existing stock.

The consideration in the

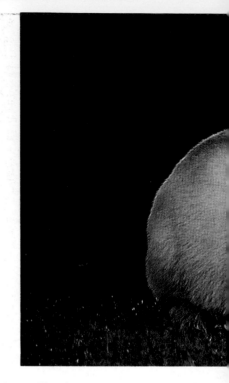

selection will, of course, depend on whether the breeding of show specimens is contemplated, in which case it will be necessary to seek out suppliers of the preferred variety. Selection of a good example of such varieties is something which is a hit-or-miss affair, until one has gained experience. It is advisable to study the standards of the particular breed, visit a few shows and observe the good points of the winners (as well as the bad points of the losers) and generally get a feel for the breed. The prospective purchase

Above: *This variety of Netherland Dwarf is identified as a Seal Point by rabbit fanciers. Photo by R. Hanson.*

should be examined for signs of disease and one of the first things to note is the general appearance and demeanor of the animal. It should be lively and show a certain amount of reluctance in being picked up. Rabbits which sit moping in a corner and allow themselves to be handled without protest should be avoided.

The coat of the animal, unless it is molting at the time, should be sleek and silky, evenly distributed on the body and free of bald patches. A coat which has a rough appearance, with fur laying in various directions, is called a *staring* coat and is an indication of poor condition, perhaps resulting from inadequate diet. Rex rabbits, in particular, are subject to sparsely covered areas of the body, often on the underside of the body and legs, so careful inspection should be made of these parts.

Ensure that the animal is breathing evenly and quietly, with no signs of wheezing or labored respiration. Obviously, if there are signs of nasal discharge, the animal will already be suffering from a respiratory infection and should be avoided. Its eyes should be bright and clear, with no sign of cataracts or dullness, which can indicate illness or old age. Rabbits with weeping eyes, inflamed eyelids and other obvious maladies should not be purchased.

The body of the animal should be thoroughly examined by passing the fingers over the skin, which should be fairly loose, but the flesh underneath should be firm and there should be no unusual lumps or protuberances which could point to any one of several unpleasant conditions. The area around the vent should be clean, and free of any fecal matter which would indicate diarrhea. Scabs or inflammation on the genitals could indicate vent disease.

As the rabbit is *sound oriented,* its sense of hearing is most important and the interior of its large, mobile ears contains a rather delicate and precise mechanism which could easily be damaged by infection. Examine the interior of the ears before purchasing and do not buy any animal which exhibits inflammation, scabs or excessive waxy deposits, all of which could mean an infection of ear canker, which is most unpleasant and highly infectious. After handling any rabbit suspected of disease, wash your hands thoroughly before proceeding to the next one.

Handling

Learning to handle rabbits correctly should be given priority and, if unsure, go to an established breeder and ask to be shown how to do it. Rabbits should **never** be picked up solely by the ears, which could cause damage to the delicate mechanism within. Always use both hands, restraining the animal by the ears or preferably the loose skin at the nape of the neck with the left hand and sliding the right hand under the chest or rump in order to gently lift it. For examining a rabbit, it is best to place it on a non-slip surface so that it does not slide about. A piece of burlap placed over a table makes an ideal surface. Young rabbits, being more nervous and flighty than most adults, are often more difficult to pick up. They may be grasped gently but firmly about the loins with one hand and then lifted with the other.

aggressive for territorial or protective reasons.

Cleaning

The most regular job to be carried out by the rabbit keeper, apart from feeding,

The correct way of holding a rabbit. Illustration by John R. Quinn.

Nervous rabbits should be held against one's chest, thus making them feel more secure and less likely to struggle. Rabbits rarely attempt to bite, though one should be wary of older adult males, and females with a litter which may occasionally become

is the cleaning out of hutches and enclosures. Hutches should be cleaned out at least twice per week, preferably at the same times and on the same days, so that the rabbits will get accustomed to these routine disturbances and will not be unduly

Cleaning

alarmed. If two days of the week are set aside for cleaning chores, Mondays and Thursdays for instance, then this will become routine and be less likely to be forgotten.

Remove the animal from the hutch when cleaning, and place it in a safe place. Never put it on a table or other elevated position where there is a danger of its falling or jumping off and injuring itself. Established tame animals can usually be placed on the floor in the vicinity of the hutch, where they will stay without restraint. Otherwise, they may be placed in an empty hutch or even a cardboard carton.

Essential equipment for cleaning out includes a scraper (a wide blade wallpaper scraper is ideal), a small shovel and a stiff handbrush. Scrape the floor litter and bedding into a pile and shovel it into a bin or sack. Pay particular attention to the corners which the animal uses to urinate or defecate and finally sweep up the remaining dust with the handbrush. The floor litter and bedding is then replaced, food and water containers washed and replaced and the animal then returned. Whether indoors or out, the areas around the hutches should be kept spotlessly clean and free of food, bedding or droppings which could attract vermin.

At monthly intervals, it is advisable to give the hutches a more thorough cleaning, using a solution of household bleach or ammonia in hot water. The whole of the inside of the hutch should be thoroughly scrubbed in the solution and then rinsed out with clean water. The chemicals will destroy any germs which have colonized the cracks and corners and remove unpleasant odors. Hutches should be dried out before the bedding and the animals are returned.

When several rabbits are kept together in hutches or enclosures, or where there is a mother and litter, it may be necessary to clean out more than twice per week. As rabbits usually soil only particular areas, it is easy to remove the soiled litter with a shovel every day and replace it with fresh material, but still maintaining the two days reserved for thorough cleaning.

Right: *The fur of white rabbits and pale colored varieties will require some attention. Photo by Hans-Joachim Richter.*

Hutch Maintenance
Hutches should be examined regularly for

Above: *A Netherland Dwarf rabbit with shaded fur. Photo by M. Gilroy.*

signs of damage which could admit drafts and water, or even result in escapes. Cracks and holes should be patched, preferably from the outside, as soon as possible. Badly fitting doors, damaged hinges and catches should also be repaired at the first opportunity. Occasionally one may have a rabbit which is a compulsive gnawer of the hutch fabric and once this habit is established, it is extremely difficult to stop it. Giving twigs may divert the animal's attention, as already discussed but it may be necessary to protect the inner edges of the hutch with galvanized steel sheeting, which can be obtained from a hardware supplier. Such sheeting can be cut into shape with tinsnips, hammered around a piece of batten to get the angle, and tacked over the vulnerable areas inside the hutch.

Once a year, preferably in the late summer or fall,

after the breeding season, hutches should be given a thorough cleaning, dried out, and repainted. It is always best to have one or more spare hutches for occasions such as this, so that the rabbits are suitably housed during the maintenance. After the timber of the hutches has thoroughly dried out, the inner surfaces should be wirebrushed to remove any loose paint and smoothed over with sandpaper. Lead-free paint should be used and some of the modern, vinyl based emulsions are ideal - they are quick drying and one coat is usually sufficient. Light colors give the best effect and, as long as the paint is thoroughly dried out, there is no danger of the animals' coats becoming soiled. The outside of the hutch should be given a coat of wood preservative.

Disposal of Manure
All soiled bedding, floor litter, waste food and droppings should be disposed of hygienically and certainly not left lying around in the vicinity of the house or the hutches. It is best to have an area in some remote corner of the garden where the manure can be dumped. Hutch scrapings can easily be

burnt and once lit will smoulder away. The ashes can be spread on the garden. Alternatively, the mixture can be added to the compost heap and allowed to rot away naturally. Rabbit manure is extremely rich in plant nutrients and much prized by gardeners. It is best to keep the compost in an enclosure which is walled in on three sides and the waste materials can be

For sanitary reasons and neat appearance, debris should not be left under the hutch indefinitely.

tipped systematically on the surface. The addition of one of the proprietary brands of composting chemicals will soon break down sawdust, hay, scraps and droppings into a first class fertilizing compost.

Nail Clipping

Grooming

Rabbits, particularly the longer haired varieties, should be groomed about once a week, which will keep their coats clean and prevent any knots forming. A medium bristle brush of the type used for long-haired cats is ideal. The coat should be brushed continuously from front to back, starting at the head and working down the back and flanks, finally turning the animal over and brushing the belly. During routine grooming, the rabbit should be inspected for any sign of disease, which will be easier to treat and cure if caught in the early stages. Angora rabbits will require a wide-toothed comb as well as a brush.

Above: *Grooming tools: all-purpose comb, fine-toothed comb, nail clippers, slicker brush, and round-tipped scissors. Photo by Bruce Crook.*

Nail Clipping

Occasionally, tame rabbits develop overgrown claws, though this is not usually a problem with animals kept on a reasonably hard surface. Overgrown claws will begin to curve and look unsightly, and there is a danger of their getting caught in cracks or in the wire mesh, causing injury. They may be clipped with normal nail clippers or strong scissors, taking care not to cut into the quick. It is best for two

persons to do this, one to restrain the animal, while the other does the clipping.

Below: *A slicker brush is used here for removing loose hairs. Hairs if swallowed in great amounts can cause intestinal blockage. Photo by Bruce Crook.*

A suggested position for cutting the claws of a rabbit. Illustration by Richard Crammer.

Identification

When one has large numbers of rabbits, it is desirable that they be marked for identification purposes. There are several ways of doing this, ranging from tatooing of the ears to metal clips which are punched through the ear. However, the most humane method, and the only one

47

recognized for exhibition purposes, is ringing of one of the hind legs. In the UK, the British Rabbit Council supplies rings of several sizes for the various breeds; each one is individually numbered and the name and address of the purchaser is recorded. The ring is placed over the hock joint of one of the hind legs when the animal is between nine and twelve weeks old. Care should be taken to ensure that the correct rings for the breed in question are used, bearing in mind that there is a great difference in the size of a Netherlands Dwarf and a Flemish Giant.

Below: An identification tattoo should be legible and situated in a part of the ear easy to see. Photo by Bruce Crook.

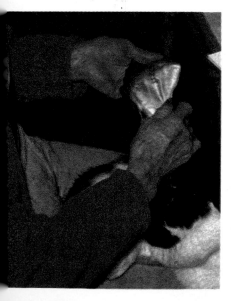

At ringing age, one should be just able to slide the ring over the joint and within a few days, it will no longer be removable. In adult rabbits, it is impossible to remove the ring without breaking it or injuring the animal but, providing it is the correct sized ring for the breed, it will cause no discomfort. A ringed rabbit bears permanent identification for life and this is a great aid to accurate record keeping.

Record Keeping
The serious breeder of rabbits will not get very far

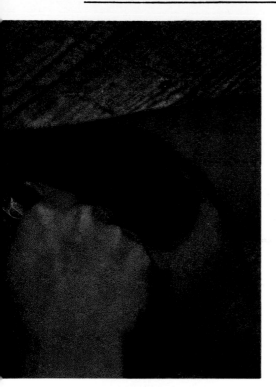

if adequate records are not kept. It is best to get into the habit of record keeping, starting with one's first breeding pair of rabbits. There are several methods of keeping records and, if all of the animals are ringed it is easy for each to have an individual record card, or page in the record book. The advent of home computers of course makes it an even simpler matter to record relevant information. The type of information recorded will include breed, sex, name, ring number, date of birth, sire, dam, when mated and to whom, number in litter

Above: *Tattooing is best performed by two persons, especially when tattooing a large and powerful rabbit. Photo by Bruce Crook.*

Below: *The club's secretary keeps all the records of entries. Proper identification of each rabbit is a must. Photo by Mervin F. Roberts.*

and any other information considered necessary or interesting. Things such as unusual traits or habits can be recorded, which may be of interest after following a number of generations. Quite often, undesirable trends can be eliminated from the breeding stock by careful study of records.

Above: An adult ringed rabbit. The ring moves freely. Photo by Michael Gilroy.

Unless identified, tracing ownership of similar looking rabbits in a show could prove difficult. Photo by David Robinson.

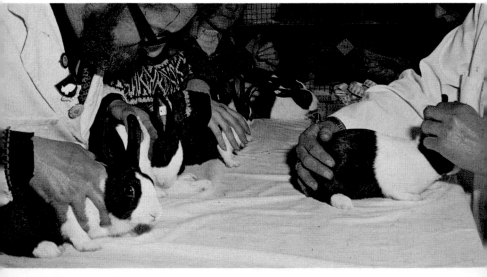

Rabbit Breeds and Varieties

It is not easy to assess the number of different rabbit breeds and varieties as different countries each have their own lists of standards which cover the recognized types. What may be a recognized breed in one country need not necessarily be in another, but there are a number of breeds which are recognized internationally as such and the most popular and well-known ones will be listed here. There is in fact a distinction between a breed and a variety. The former refers to the size and form of the animal, while the latter refers to one of the several colors or combinations of colors which exist within the breed.

It is not possible to state with any accuracy when individual breeds first started. Rabbits were initially bred for meat and fur and it is known that forms of the Lop and the Angora existed in England towards the end of the 18th century, although it was five or six decades later that exhibiting for competitive purposes began to develop. During this time, most of the popular 'old' breeds were developed and have remained to the present.

Batches of new varieties are recognized at regular intervals, while some of the older ones may become extinct, due to a lull in popularity.

In color and size, wild rabbits look alike. The wild coloration provides a camouflaging effect for eluding predators.

There are three ways in which a new breed may be produced: by selective breeding of animals with outstanding characteristics through several generations, until a strain differing greatly from the original stock is produced; by combining the characteristics in two or more breeds; or by exploiting the occasional mutation which may appear. In the latter case, a mutation is a rare case in which new characteristics appear, when the mechanism which controls the inherited characteristics behaves abnormally. Such mutations may take the form of change in color, type of coat or body shape. A good example of such a mutation is the Rex rabbit, a variety in which the stiff guard hairs in the coat are reduced to the length of the undercoat hairs, producing a beautiful, velvet-like fur.

For exhibition purposes, domestic rabbits may be loosely divided into two categories, the Fancy Breeds and the Fur Breeds. The latter is further sub-divided into the Rexes, the Sables and the Satins.

Fancy Breeds

The Angora: This is a very old breed which is unmistakable in appearance, its long fluffy coat making it appear twice its real size. It is the only breed which is kept exclusively for wool production and, in some countries, notably France and Japan, quite a major industry has arisen. The high quality wool is much in demand for the manufacture of hats,

Below: *Ample furnishings on the ears identifies this longhaired white rabbit as an English Angora.*

jumpers and other garments, which fetch considerable prices. The Angora is a medium sized rabbit averaging 3 kg (about 6½ lb) in weight and the coat may be any of twelve color varieties, on the head is shorter and may be slightly curly. There are prominent tufts at the ear tips.

although white (albino) is by far the most popular. The fine, soft coat stands out from the body, but that

Anyone considering the possibility of keeping Angoras should first ensure that the time and

Above: *The French Angora is another recognized longhaired breed. Photo by Vince Serbin.*

will cause matting problems and irritation to the animals. Another problem is compaction of hair in the gut, caused by the rabbit eating its shed fur. Before clipping, the coat should be thoroughly combed, and a parting made along the spinal column. It is usually best to have two people performing the clipping operation, one to hold the rabbit, while the other is doing the snipping. The wool should be clipped to within 1 cm (1/2 in) of the skin, but no closer. A sharp watch should be kept for the teats of the doe, when clipping the wool on the belly, to avoid accidental injury.

The Belgian Hare: Although there are several myths that this breed originated from the wild hare, it is a true rabbit and has no connection with the other species, although there is certainly a resemblance in size and body shape. The long, lanky body and legs give the breed a 'racy appearance' and the short coat is invariably a rich, deep chestnut in color. At one time, the Belgian Hare was much used in meat production, particularly during World War II when it

the patience are available. The animals require thorough grooming at least once a week and failure to do this will result in intense matting and knotting of the fur. Whether being kept for wool or not, the coat must be clipped back at least once a year (commercial keepers shear their rabbits about four times a year and expect an annual wool yield of at least 350 gm (12 oz) per rabbit, per year), preferably in the summer months; otherwise the molt was often crossed with other breeds to improve weight. It is now bred almost exclusively for exhibition and pet stock. The average weight of an adult is around 4 kg (9 lb). It is an active animal, and requires lots of exercise to keep its muscles in trim. Access to outside runs, or regular 'walks' on the lawn

Below: *A general appearance of alertness is characteristic of a Belgian Hare.*

varieties, the Dutch Rabbit, as may be expected, originated in the Netherlands. The early precursors of the breed, which arrived in Britain in the 1830's, were known as 'Little Brabancons' and it was not long before the Dutch breed, as we know it, became a recognized form. There are a number of color varieties, including black, blue, chocolate, gray, tortoiseshell and

are therefore essential. It is an intelligent, graceful and endearing rabbit, which makes a splendid pet, providing one has the space to house and excercise it.

Dutch: One of the most popular of the fancy

yellow, the first two being the most popular. The front half of the body is white, the hind part colored and the dividing line should be as straight as possible. The head and ears are also colored, but a blaze of white extends from the nose, up to a point between the ears. The average weight of the Dutch is around 2 kg (4½ lb) and, although small, it was formerly used for meat production, particularly when crossed with larger breeds. The Dutch is now a major pet and exhibition breed which frequently does well on the show bench. One exciting aspect of breeding Dutch rabbits is that one can clearly see the markings on the young, almost as soon as they are born.

English: The English is one of the oldest fancy breeds and is known from the early part of the 19th century. It vies with the Dutch for popularity and is another breed often seen on the show bench. The ground color of the English is white and it may be marked with black, blue, chocolate, gray or tortoiseshell. The markings appear as small blotches on the nose, around the eyes and along the flanks, while a continuous, narrow stripe extends down the spinal ridge, from the neck to the base of the tail. Breeding the English presents a challenge, as the ideal show specimens must have spots and stripes of the correct size, shape and position! The

English rabbit averages 3 kg (6½ lb) in weight and makes an excellent pet, being trusting and docile. The does make ideal foster

Below: A Dutch rabbit is considered perfect when the demarcation between white and colored areas is straight and unbroken. Photo by Vince Serbin.

mothers, readily accepting a litter of its own, or other breeds.

The Flemish Giant: This really is the true giant of the rabbit fancy and animals weighing as much as 10 kg (22 lb) have been exhibited, although a more average weight is 5 kg (12 lb) for bucks, and 6 kg (14 lb) for does. In the UK, the only recognized color variety is steel-gray, although several other colors are recognized in

the USA. In spite of its name, it is almost certain that the Flemish Giant originated in Britain and probably descended from the Patagonian, a breed which is now extinct. It was

probably first developed primarily for meat production, as it is a fast grower and gave quick results. It is a much loved exhibition rabbit and also makes a good pet, though the occasional buck can be a little pugnacious.

Harlequin: Aptly named, the Harlequin has a brindling of stripes which may come in several varieties. Black and yellow is the most usual, but chocolate and yellow, blue and cream or black and white are also possible. The latter is sometimes called the Magpie. It is said to have originated in France, towards the end of the last century.

Himalayan: Another popular fancy breed, the Himalayan is a medium sized rabbit with an average adult weight of about 2.3 kg (5 lb). The body is white with the exception of the ears, nose and feet. The technical term for these areas of color are the 'points' and they may be black, blue, chocolate or lilac. The Himalayan is one of the oldest fancy breeds and is thought to have originated in the Far East. In continental Europe it is known as the 'Russian' and

Fancy Breeds

at one time in Britain, it was known as the 'Chinese'. Technically, the Himalayan is an albino, and indeed, the coloring of the points only begins to develop on the young after they have left the nest. It is said that the coloring on the extremities is caused by minute differences in temperature, and that pigmentation will develop on other parts of the body which are regularly bathed with iced water. The Himalayan is a very docile breed which makes an excellent pet.

Below: *Harlequins have been bred in many color combinations and fur types, but perfect specimens are rarely seen. Photo by Ray Hanson.*

The Lop: This is another old breed which was probably developed in England at the beginning of the 19th century. The outstanding feature of the Lop is its enormous ears which may reach a span of 70 cm (28 in), and there is much competition among

Above: *Netherland Dwarf rabbits available in many colors and markings. Photo by Michael Gilroy.*

breeders to produce specimens with ears of the ideal length, breadth and shape. The average adult Lop weighs about 3 kg (61/2 lb) and may be almost any color. There are two sub-breeds, the French and the Dwarf, both of which are less popular than the standard breed which is normally referred to as the English Lop. The Lop is docile and makes a good pet, but its bedding must be kept scrupulously clean, so that the ears do not become soiled. The Lop has been regularly used as a laboratory

probably developed from the Polish, another small breed, in Holland during the 1930's but it was not widely known until after the war. With the exception of the Dutch and the English, this is the most popular exhibition breed. They come in a variety of colors, including black, brown, chinchilla, gray, himalayan, smoke-pearl, white and many others. This is a compact little rabbit with short, pointed ears and due to its diminutive size, very popular as a pet.

Above: *The points or markings of a good Himalayan rabbit should be distinct. Photo by Michael Gilroy.*

animal, due to the ease in which blood samples may be taken from the large blood vessels in the ear.

Netherland Dwarf: This is the smallest rabbit breed, average adult weight being less than 1 kg (2 lb), and not much larger than a guinea pig, an animal with which it will live in community. The Netherland Dwarf was

Fancy Breeds

Polish: This is another small breed although a little larger than the Netherland Dwarf, the average adult weight being around 1.2 kg (2½ lb). Like the other dwarf, the breed comes in a great number of colors, but the red-eyed white seems to be the most popular. The origin of this breed is not documented, but it probably arose from Dutch or English during the latter

Below: When shown a Polish rabbit should sit upright, head held high, and ears erect. Photo by Ray Hanson.

The red-eyed white Netherland Dwarf is the most popular of the many different colors of Netherland Dwarfs available. Photo by Burkhard Kahl.

half of the 19th century, at which time they were considerably larger than their modern counterparts.

Silver: This is a medium sized breed, weighing about 3 kg (6 lbs) when adult. The ground color

Right: Ticking of the hairs results in a beautiful and attractive silver gray effect on the black coat. Photo by Michael Gilroy.

Above: *The Dwarf Lop rabbit is also called Holland Lop on account of the contribution of the Netherland Dwarf breed. Photo by Bruce Crook.*

exhibition rabbits and also make very good pets.

Tan: A very attractive breed, the Tan comes in black, blue, chocolate or lilac with a tan, or yellow colored belly. It is said that the first Tans were produced accidentally by mixing domesticated rabbits with wild stock during the 1880's. With an average adult weight of about 2 kg (4½ lb), the Tan is a popular exhibition breed, often seen on the show benches.

may be black, yellow or agouti and the silver ticking (consisting of white flecks in the hairs) makes respectively, the silver-gray, the fawn and the brown varieties of this breed. At birth, the young rabbits exhibit only the ground coloring and it is only after the first molt that the silvering appears, usually at about six weeks of age. Silvers are popular

The Fur Breeds

Alaska: A relatively new breed, the Alaska originated in Germany. Its self-colored black coat is tight and glossy.

Argenté: This breed was developed in France, primarily for fur production and, at one time, its pelts raised high prices. The Argenté Champagne is the largest of the varieties,

Below: *If shown this English rabbit could be faulted for having incomplete eye circles. Photo by Ray Hanson.*

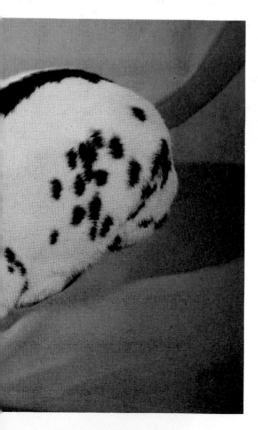

Above: *A Bleu Argente rabbit in a rabbit competition. Photo courtesy of the Texas Agricultural Extension Service.*

weighing an average of 3.5 kg (8 lb). The color of this variety is basically blue-black, with heavy white flecking in the undercoat. Other varieties of the breed are the Argenté Bleu, with a ground color of lavender blue and weighing about 3 kg (6 lb); the Argenté Brun, with a ground color of brown and weighing the same as the Bleu; and Argenté Creme, the smallest of the group weighing about 2.5 kg (5 lb) with a ground color of orange-yellow. Like the Silvers, Argentés are born with the ground color only, taking on the silvering after the first molt.

being a good exhibition rabbit. Weighing approximately 3.2 kg (7½ lb), the most popular colors are blue or white, but black or brown varieties may occasionally be seen. The Beveren is a

Above: A Beveren is a large and meaty rabbit. Its hair can grow to a length of one and a quarter inches. Photo by Ray Hanson.

quality fur breed, with a thick lustrous coat up to 3 cm (1¼ in) in length.

Beveren: This breed, which originated in Belgium, is a fine example of a general purpose animal, suitable for meat and fur production as well as

Californian: This breed was developed in the USA primarily for meat and fur production and probably originated from the Himalayan, which it resembles, being white

with colored points. It is, however, much heavier, a good specimen weighing as much as 4 kg (11 lb). Two point colors are recognized, black and chocolate. The breed did not arrive in Europe until the late 1950's, when it soon became a regular visitor to the show bench.

Examining the distribution of pigments and texture of a Chinchilla rabbit's coat. Photo by David Robinson.

The Chinchilla: This breed was named after the wild *Chinchilla lanigera,* a South American animal much sought after for its pelt which has always commanded high prices.

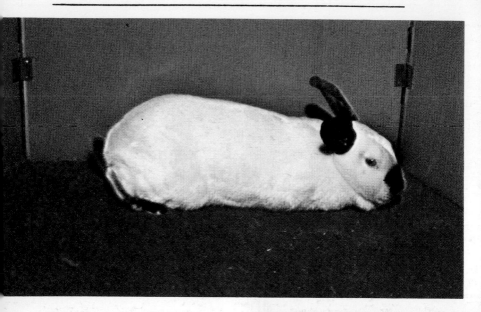

The Chinchilla rabbit was bred to imitate the fur of its more expensive cousin and, as a rather good facsimile was produced, this breed has commanded high popularity for fur production. The original Chinchilla was first bred in France in the early part of this century, reputedly by crossing wild rabbits with Blue Beverens and Himalayans, but there seems to be some dispute arising from this claim. In the Chinchilla, the yellow color in the wild agouti coat has been replaced by pearl. An average adult weighs about 3 kg (6½ lb).

The Chinchilla Giganta: Due to the popularity of the Chinchilla pelt, attempts to breed a larger version

Left: *The Californian is now bred the world over for meat and fur. Photo courtesy of the Texas Agricultural Service.*

resulted in the Chinchilla Giganta, a rabbit weighing up to 5 kg (11 lb). This is an ideal meat and fur breed with a coat slightly darker in color and somewhat coarser than in the original Chinchilla.

Below: *A good Chinchilla rabbit can receive 30 and 35 points for coat quality and color. Photo by Michael Gilroy.*

The Fox: A medium sized fur breed weighing about 2.7 kg (6 lb), the first Foxes were exhibited in 1926. These were Black Foxes, with a black ground color, white belly and considerable white ticking along the flanks. This variety is sometimes also referred to as the Silver Fox. Other varieties now include Blue Fox, Chocolate Fox and Lilac Fox. This highly attractive breed is popular as an exhibition subject.

The Havana: A medium sized, self-colored breed, the Havana was first developed in Holland around the turn of the century. The fur is a rich, chocolate color, the darker the better and the eyes are ruby red. It has previously been much in demand as a fur breed.

The Lilac: The lilac color is really a dove-gray which is a dilute brown, first produced at Cambridge, England in 1922. A docile and friendly rabbit, the Lilac reaches about 3 kg (6½ lb) in weight. Specimens produced in Europe may still be referred to as Gouda, or Marbourg, after the district

Above: *Note the unusually beautiful and thick coat of this Havana Rex. Photo by Photo by David Robinson.*

in which they were developed.

New Zealand Black and New Zealand White: Both of these breeds were developed in the USA, primarily for meat production. Fast growing, the adults average 4 kg (9 lb). The colors are self black and albino (red-eyed white).

New Zealand Red: There is some confusion over the origin of this breed. A form of it was certainly developed in the USA in 1909, either from stock imported from New Zealand or, more likely, from mutation Flemish Giants, crossed with Belgian Hares. The American version is a large rabbit, weighing about 4.1 kg (9 lb), whereas the British form weighs considerably less. The coat is dark, orange-red in color and not suitable for fur, due to its harshness.

Rex Rabbits: These constitute a category of rabbit which revolutionized the pelt industry. It first appeared in 1919 and was found by M. Caillon, a Frenchman, in a litter from an ordinary gray doe. As a buck and a doe were included in the litter, they were bred together and soon a small stock was handed to a priest, Abbé Gillet, who continued to nurture the breed. Rex rabbits were exhibited for the first time at the Paris International Show in 1924 and by 1930, they had found their way into many other countries. The first variety was known as a Castor Rex, this being an agouti type, of a dark-chestnut color. The Rex character is one in which the long, stiff, guard hairs

Below: *The New Zealand White are strong rabbits, and may prove difficult to handle as a pet by children.*

are shortened and weakened through mutation, giving the fur an appearance of uniform thickness and length, all over the body. Such a quality was soon sought after by furriers and the breeders began to improve the quality of the coat, and increase the number of varieties by selective breeding. It is now possible to get almost every known breed of rabbit with the Rex characteristics, the most popular being Black, Blue, Brown, Chinchilla, Havana, Himalayan, and Sable. Even fancy breeds such as the Dutch and the English are available in Rex form. Two unusual varieties are the Astrex, which has a wavy coat, and the Opossum Rex with fur up to 2.5 cm (1 in) in length.

Above: *A Lilac Rex rabbit; the fur is dove-gray with excellent density. Photo courtesy of the Texas Agricultural Extension Service.*

Most Rex rabbits are of the medium sized range.

The Sable: This breed comes in two varieties, the Siamese and the Marten. The colors are a blend of dark and light sepia-brown tones. In the Siamese the dark color of the black shades into lighter tones along the flanks and belly. The Marten has white ticking along the flanks and a white belly. The coat of the Sable is of high quality and is much sought after by furriers. It is a medium sized breed, weighing about 2.7 kg (6 lb).

Right: *A Netherland Dwarf rabbit with color shadings of a Marten Sable. Photo by Michael Gilroy.*

The Fur Breeds

The Satin: This breed arose as the result of a mutation similar in origin to the Rex. It was first developed in the USA in 1930, but did not arrive in Europe until 1947. The outstanding feature of the mutation was the satin-like glossiness of the coat, caused by a flattening of the hair scales and an absence or scarcity of the central hollow cells found in normal hairs. The most popular color variety is the Ivory (an albino type), but

The Siberian: First developed in 1930, the Siberian was produced to provide matching pelts of uniform color for the fur trade. However, the breed never attained the popularity which was hoped for in this aspect. The breed comes in a range of self colors, and is occasionally seen on the show bench.

The Smoke Pearl: These were first produced from

Above: *The satin factor adds sheen and lustre to a Chinchilla rabbit's coat. Photo courtesy of the Texas Agricultural Extension Service.*

many other colors are available. The Satins are medium sized rabbits, weighing about 3.2 kg (7 lb).

Sables in the late 1920's and soon became extremely popular. The back is dark, smoky brown, merging into light beige on the flanks. The face, ears and feet are also dark in color. The Marten type has a white underside and lateral white ticking.

Above: *This Siamese Sable Satin is considered to be of good type and sheen. Photo by David Robinson.*

Below: *A Brittania Petite (English Polish) with Smoke Pearl color pattern. Photo by David Robinson.*

Health and Hygiene

A healthy animal is one that is in prime condition, both physically and mentally, which in the rabbit manifests itself in sleekness of coat, brightness of eyes and general *joie de vivre*. While in such condition, the animal is best able to ward off the effects of infectious diseases due to its resistance being in peak form. Hygiene is the science of the prevention of diseases and, as with any animals kept in close confinement, only stringent hygienic measures coupled with correct husbandry, will ensure that stock remains in a healthy condition.

Any animal which is not healthy is either suffering from a communicable disease or a non-communicable condition. The former is a disease caused by any number of types of parasitic organism, such as bacteria, viruses, protozoa, helminths (worms) or external arthropodal parasites (e.g. mites, lice, fleas) and which may be transmitted from one animal to another in a number of ways, sometimes causing an outbreak or epidemic. The latter is a state of unhealthiness, caused by a number of conditions, not transmittable from animal to animal and includes such things as nutritional disturbances, injuries, hypothermia, heatstroke and minor ailments like overgrown claws or teeth.

There are four major methods by which communicable diseases are transmitted among rabbits, and a knowledge of these will help the keeper to keep disease out of the stock.

1. Airborne: These are usually respiratory infections; the organisms are taken into the respiratory tract during normal breathing. The infected animal will cough and sneeze, sending out droplets of mucus containing millions of the disease organisms which are then inhaled by another animal. An example of such a disease in rabbits is snuffles.

2. Enteric: These are usually infections of the alimentary system and the organisms are taken in with food or water which have been contaminated with the feces, or sometimes the urine of the infected animal. Food may be directly contaminated with the droppings of infected rabbits, or indirectly by flies

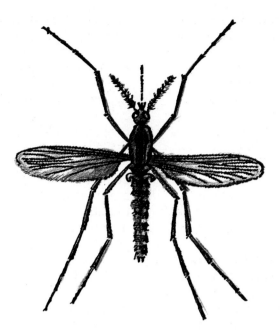

Dorsal view of an adult mosquito.

transmitting the organisms from droppings to food or even by the hands of the rabbit keeper. A good example of such a disease is coccidiosis.

3. Vector: These are usually infections of the blood and internal organs and are transmitted from one animal to the next by bloodsucking parasites, such as fleas, lice, mites and even mosquitoes. Biting parasites usually inject an anti-coagulant saliva into the wound before sucking up a blood meal and it is at this stage that organisms of an infected animal from a previous meal are introduced into the victim. An example of such a disease is myxomatosis, transmitted by the rabbit flea.

4. Contact: These are usually diseases of the skin, or mucus membranes and are spread by direct physical contact. A good example is venereal or vent disease.

In spite of the many ways in which diseases are transmitted, domestic rabbits remain surprisingly free of ailments, providing a few simple rules of

hygiene are followed. Control of respiratory infections can be accomplished by ensuring that the animals get adequate ventilation, without unnecessary drafts. This particularly applies to rabbits kept indoors. In any case, all rabbits should receive regular fresh air and exercise - either a run on the lawn, or a stint in a Morant pen will be good for them.

Sick rabbits should always be isolated from the other stock, in a separate room if these are indoors. After handling sick animals, *always* wash the hands thoroughly before touching other

Above: *Water bottles should be cleaned regularly and only safe drinking water given. Photo by Dr. Herbert R. Axelrod.*

stock, food, bedding or utensils. Never move items from the hutch of a sick animal to that of healthy stock. Any new animals purchased or obtained should be given a period of quarantine, for at least fourteen days before being introduced to the other stock. During the quarantine period, careful watch should be kept on the newcomer to ensure that no disease is developing. If all is well after the quarantine period, it is unlikely that any disease will have been brought in.

Inadequate diet is one of the surest ways to trigger an outbreak of disease in captive stock. The moment an animal begins to suffer malnutrition, its defenses against pathogenic organisms (which are all around us) break down and it is likely to get an infection secondary to that caused by the dietary deficiency. Nutrition has been discussed in an earlier chapter and is important to ensure that the animals receive a balanced diet if disease is to be avoided.

Disease Recognition

It is not always immediately apparent when a rabbit is ailing, although there are various signs which will indicate the beginnings of an infection. Obviously, if treatment is to be successful, it is imperative to catch the disease in its early stages. It is therefore important to inspect one's stock regularly and

Below: *When housing rabbits in a single pen, the sex, age, size and temperament of each individual should be considered. Adults in season should be caged apart.*

frequently, preferably at least twice per week, if not daily. A fancier who regularly handles his stock and gets to know each individual is much more likely to recognize signs of ill health than the person who just looks upon the feeding and cleaning as an undesirable chore.

The usual first signs of sickness in a rabbit are that it will sit hunched up in a corner, its hair often standing out, and it will not react to the usual stimuli. Diagnosis and treatment of all but the commonest complaints are not for the fancier, but for the veterinarian who should be consulted as soon as possible. It is better to have a sick rabbit diagnosed and treated (or even destroyed) rather than risk an epidemic breaking out in one's whole stock.

There are a number of diseases and conditions which may occur in the domestic rabbit and the ones most frequently encountered are listed here:

Abscesses: These may be felt as a soft lump under the rabbit's skin when the hand is passed over the body. Abscesses arise when the bacteria or other pathogenic organisms of one or more types enter the skin via external injuries, which may have been caused by fighting, or by catching the skin on projecting wire or nails. Quite often the wound will be too small to notice and it is only when the abscess develops that it becomes apparent. Left untreated, abscesses can become an enormous size and could result in the death of the animal. Caught in the early stages however, they are relatively easy to cure. To treat a small abscess, the fur around it should be gently cut away, using a pair of sharp scissors. The abscess is then gently bathed in warm water containing antiseptic, of a dilution as recommended by the manufacturer. The scab formed over the site of the injury can usually be worked loose with prolonged bathing and the contents of the pustule gently squeezed out. After the wound has been emptied of pus, it is again bathed with antiseptic solution and then wiped dry. An antiseptic cream can then be applied to the area, as well as getting some of this into the wound itself.

In the case of very large abscesses, or where there is some difficulty in

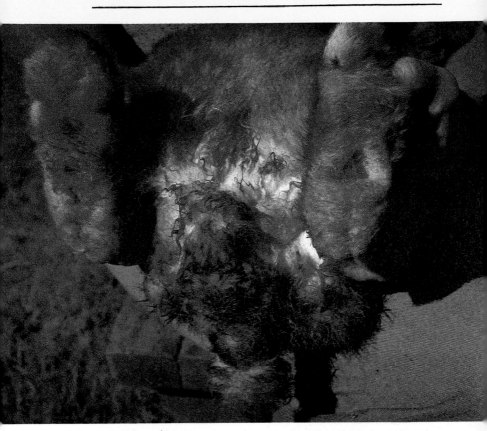

removing the pus, a veterinarian should be consulted, who will probably perform simple surgery and prescribe antibiotic treatment. Sometimes hard lumps may be felt under the skin; these are usually benign tumors which the veterinarian can often successfully remove by minor surgery.

Bloat: This is a really nasty attack of 'gas', usually caused by overindulgence in certain types of green food, but occasionally

Above: *The irritated vent area and sore hock on this rabbit resulted from unsanitary hutch conditions. Photo by Bruce Cook.*

appearing with no apparent explanation. A rabbit suffering from bloat will be experiencing severe pain, and will usually sit hunched up, looking miserable. By gently squeezing the belly of the bloated animal, it will be found to have a drum-like tautness. Bloat can mainly be avoided by not giving the rabbit excessive amounts of greenstuff,

particularly of a type which it is not used to receiving regularly. When introducing a new kind of green food, it should first be given in very small quantities and built up gradually. Bloat is caused by excessive production of gases in the animal's gut, usually the lower intestine, and is due to unnatural fermentation of foods. A rabbit suffering from this condition should immediately have its green food discontinued and should be fed sparingly on

Above: Discourage random feeding. Children could unwittingly give too much of the wrong kind of food.

a little dry food. A dose of kaolin or bicarbonate of soda dissolved in water can be given from a spoon. The treatment should continue daily until the bloat has subsided, when the animal may be gradually brought back to its normal diet.

Right: Rabbits dislike sudden changes in their diet. Changes in types of food should be made gradually. Photo by Michael Gilroy.

Canker: Having particularly large and delicate ears, rabbits are occasionally prone to infection from microscopic, parasitic mites, which enter the ears and burrow into the sensitive skin lining. Mites reproduce prolifically and soon cause areas of intense inflammation which irritate the rabbits greatly. The first signs are that the animal will continually shake its head and scratch its ears. On examination, reddish inflamed areas will be seen, and if untreated, these will develop into crusty lesions. Mite infestations are transmitted from one animal to the next, and are

Inspecting and cleaning the ears on a regular basis lessens the chances of having mites settling in the ears. Photo by Bruce Crook.

usually brought into a rabbitry by a newcomer which has not been properly inspected and quarantined.

The insides of the ears of an infected animal should be bathed with a solution of antiseptic in warm water and the crusts dissolved away. The area is then dabbed dry and a proprietary miticide dusted or painted on. Commercial miticides or special canker treatments are available from your pet shop or veterinarian and usually contain benzyl benzoate, a chemical particularly effective against mites. In the case of severe secondary infection, it is advisable to consult a veterinarian, as antibiotic treatment may be necessary. After an outbreak, all hutches should be thoroughly cleaned and disinfected, preferably with a blow torch used with caution.

Coccidiosis: At one time, this disease was the dread of the commercial rabbit keeper, as it could often mean the loss of a complete stock. It is a highly serious disease, which will spread rapidly through the stock and in its later stages, is almost impossible to cure. Thankfully, due to modern methods of hygiene and treatment, the disease is not now considered to be the danger it used to be. Coccidiosis comes in two forms, one of which attacks the walls of the intestine, causing intense pain to the animal, the

Dorsal view of the canker mite of rabbit.

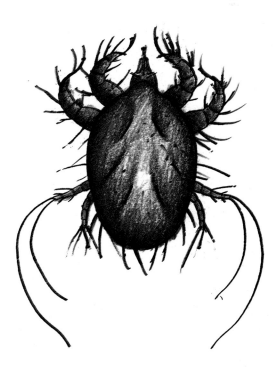

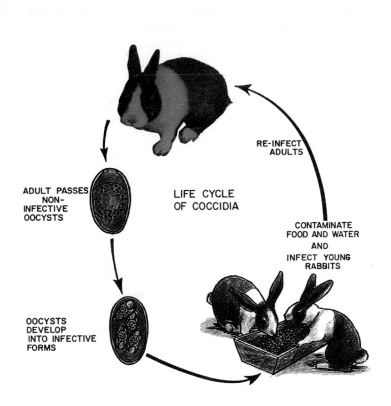

LIFE CYCLE
OF COCCIDIA

ADULT PASSES
NON-
INFECTIVE
OOCYSTS

RE-INFECT
ADULTS

CONTAMINATE
FOOD AND WATER
AND
INFECT YOUNG
RABBITS

OOCYSTS
DEVELOP
INTO INFECTIVE
FORMS

*The life cycle of coccidia is
illustrated here.*

other attacking the liver
(hepatic coccidiosis). An
infected animal will lose its
appetite, rapidly lose
weight and condition and
suffer from intense watery
diarrhea. Death will usually
follow, unless the disease
is caught in its very early
stages and treated by a
veterinarian.

As this is such a
dangerous disease,
prevention is far better
than cure. It is transmitted
from animal to animal by
infected droppings (enteric
disease). Particular care
must be taken when
cleaning the hutch, and
overcrowding must always
be avoided. Again the
importance of quarantining
new animals must be
stressed. Green food
which has been collected
from areas colonized by
wild rabbits should never
be used as this is a
common source of

infection. Sometimes adult rabbits can be carriers of the disease, without any obvious symptoms, and it is usually such a case which is responsible for a sudden outbreak of coccidiosis in a litter of young, having been infected by inadvertently eating food contaminated by the mother. In the event of a single case of the disease occurring in a stud, it is wise to take precautionary treatment measures throughout the whole stock, as advised by your veterinarian.

Colds: Rabbits are susceptible to upper respiratory infections of the type collectively referred to as colds. Symptoms include

Below: *Bob Bennet, well known rabbit expert, showing correct way of holding a rabbit. Photo by Vince Serbin.*

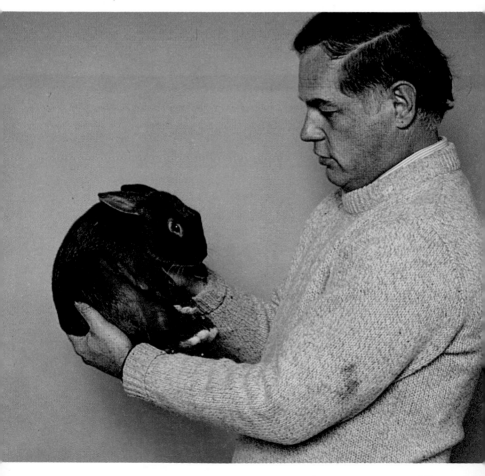

coughing, sneezing, nasal discharge, loss of appetite and lethargy. Sick animals should be isolated, kept warm, dry and draft free. The veterinarian may recommend treatment with a mild antibiotic. Rabbits normally recover well from minor infections of this sort.

Compaction of the Gut: Long haired rabbits, in particular Angoras, are susceptible to this condition and even short haired varieties may occasionally suffer. The condition is caused by a ball of fur forming somewhere in the gut, often in the duodenum, as a result of the rabbit's efforts in cleaning its body, particularly at the time of the molt. Sometimes these balls are of sufficient size to block the passage of food completely, thus causing eventual anemia and emaciation. The administration of a purgative such as castor oil will often lubricate the compaction sufficiently to cause it to move on through the system. Serious cases may be referred to the veterinarian.

Conjunctivitis: This is an infection of the eye, and the mucus membranes surrounding the eye. Symptoms include reddening of the eyes, inflammation of the eyelids and weeping. Such infections can usually be cleared up quickly and satisfactorily, using one of the excellent eye ointments or drops available from your veterinarian.

Constipation: Lack of adequate green food and vegetables, or a preponderance of fibre in the dry food will cause constipation in the rabbit. It is simple to treat by giving extra green food and fresh vegetables. In a severe case, a purgative such as castor oil can be administered.

Enteritis: This is an inflammation of the intestines which may be caused by any of a number of kinds of pathogenic organisms, ranging from the obscure and mild to some quite severe forms of Salmonellosis. Sometimes certain enteric infections can be confused with coccidiosis as the symptoms may be similar. All enteric diseases are transmitted via the food and from the droppings of other infected animals. Certain animals may act as

carriers, showing no symptoms and suffering no discomfort, while others may suddenly succumb to the infection, often as a result of the resistance being lowered by other factors, such as cold and damp, inadequate diet or physical injury. The safest course to take in an outbreak of diarrhea is to consult a veterinarian, who will be able to diagnose the disease from a fecal sample and treat accordingly.

External Parasites: There are a number of external parasites which may attack

Above: *Appearance of a rabbit in molt. At this stage grooming is essential. Photo by Bruce Crook.*

rabbits. Most of these are insects or arachnids and live from the rabbit's blood, using their biting or piercing mouthparts. Not only do parasites cause irritation and discomfort to the animals, but large numbers of blood-sucking pests can take so much blood as to cause anemia and subsequent loss of resistance to other diseases. In addition, certain parasites are capable of injecting pathogenic organisms directly into the bloodstream of rabbits during their blood meal. Fleas and lice are insects which live in the fur of the animals but can also move from one animal to the next. Infestation usually results in excessive scratching by the rabbits and obvious discomfort. Insecticidal dusting powders may be obtained from the pet dealer, and should be applied to the animal, the hutches and the bedding. It is advisable to repeat the treatment after ten days, to allow for any parasite eggs which may have hatched in the interim period.

Mites, similar to the type which cause ear canker, may sometimes attack the skin on other parts of the body, causing a condition known as mange.

The first signs are bald patches on the skin, where the hair has fallen out. In the later stages, inflammation and encrustation will occur, possibly followed by secondary infection. Treatment is as for ear canker; the infected areas are bathed, dried and treated with a benzyl benzoate preparation. Occasionally a larger relative of the mite, the tick, will be found attached to the rabbit's skin. Fortunately, ticks do not come in such large numbers and will usually occur only as single specimens. Until bloated with blood ticks are not always apparent but, when well fed, appear as gray globes about the size of a pea. The visible part is the abdomen of the tick and if one tries to pull it off it may separate from the head which is embedded in the skin. The tick will die, but the head may cause secondary infection. The best way to remove one is to dab it with alcohol (even whisky or gin will do), which will cause the tick to relax its mouthparts, when it can be removed and destroyed.

Heat Stroke: A rabbit which has been left in full sun in a stifling hutch, or perhaps for several hours in a travelling box on a hot day, will be susceptible to heat stroke. Of course, if proper care has been taken this condition should never happen but accidents do occur and it is wise to know what to do should the situation arise. A rabbit suffering from heat stroke will lie stretched out, will feel hot to the touch and will be panting heavily, sometimes

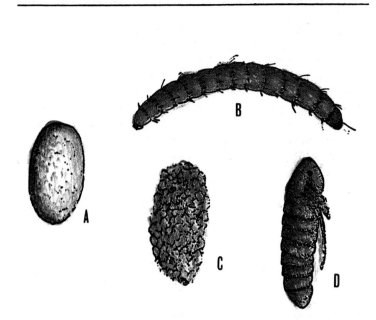

Stages in the life cycle of a flea. A. Egg. B. Larva. C. Cocoon. D. Pupa.

Lateral view of an adult flea.

foaming at the mouth. The animal should immediately be taken to a cool, shady, well ventilated place and given cool green food and cold water. In most cases the animal will recover in an hour or so, and care should be taken to ensure that the situation does not recur.

Injuries: Accidental injuries may be caused by a variety of things and can include broken bones, open wounds and internal injuries. Most are

Above: *A playful skirmish with the house cat can result in minor cuts. Wounds must be treated right away. Photo by Bruce Crook.*

preventable as long as common sense prevails. The main cause of open wounds is fighting between bucks and prevention is obvious: do not keep bucks together. Very occasionally rabbits may injure themselves on the wire of the hutch or on a protruding nail. Wounds should be bathed with antiseptic solution and a little antiseptic cream applied. Healing should take place in a short period. Larger flesh wounds may require surgical suturing by a veterinarian. Other forms of injuries may be caused by falling out of a faulty hutch door, off a table or by being dropped. Young rabbits are most susceptible to fractures but they will mend quite successfully if splinted. It is best to consult a vet. When allowed the free run of the lawn, care should be taken to see that the rabbits are not attacked by marauding cats or dogs. If not actually killed by such animals, a rabbit could be very severely injured.

Malocclusion of the Teeth: This is a condition in which the upper and lower incisor teeth are misaligned; natural wear does not occur and the teeth continue to grow to such a length that the animal is no longer able to eat. Overgrown teeth may be clipped back by a vet and sometimes a single clipping may cure the problem; however the kindest thing to do with a rabbit suffering chronically from this condition is to resort to euthanasia.

Below: *Your pet dog if properly trained may not harm your rabbit, but bites from strange dogs may prove dangerous. Photo by Bruce Crook.*

Disease Recognition

Mastitis: An unpleasant condition which occasionally affects a female rabbit, mastitis is a bacterial infection of the mammary glands which causes them to swell and become painful. An infected doe will lose her appetite but may drink large quantities of water. Treat the teats by gently massaging a little antiseptic cream into them. The veterinarian may recommend an injection of antibiotic which will normally effect a cure within a few days.

Middle Ear Disease: Sometimes called torticollis, or wry-neck, this is an infection of the balance mechanism of the middle ear, which will initially cause the rabbit to hold its head to one side. Untreated, the animal will lose its equilibrium altogether and roll over constantly. This may be a secondary infection associated with such conditions as ear canker or respiratory infections. Treatment with antibiotics will usually effect a cure.

Myxomatosis: This unpleasant disease of wild rabbits, fortunately, is rarely encountered among domestic stock. However, the danger is there, in areas where wild rabbits are close at hand. The disease manifests itself in swelling up of the eyelids, blindness, lethargy and delirium. Death will swiftly follow and, as it is almost impossible to treat, it is best to put infected animals out of their misery. As the virus causing the disease is transmitted by biting insects, notably rabbit fleas, the question of prevention lies in keeping biting insects away from your stock by strict measures of hygiene.

Pneumonia: This is any infection of the lungs, caused by one of several kinds of pathogenic organisms, often occurring as a secondary effect to untreated upper respiratory infections such as snuffles or heavy colds. Pneumonia causes the lungs to become congested with mucus, labored breathing and eventual death through lack of oxygen. If respiratory infections are caught and treated in their early stages, pneumonia is

Right: *Appearance of normal front teeth. They are aligned and straight. Photo by Vince Serbin.*

unlikely to become a problem, though it may sometimes by cured with the administration of antibiotics.

Pseudotuberculosis: This disease is so named as the symptoms resemble those of tuberculosis, down to the finest detail; however, it is caused by a completely different organism. It is a bacterial disease, which can spread into domestic stock through food contaminated by mice or rats. The control of vermin is therefore an important preventive measure. Symptoms include loss of weight, condition, and labored breathing, followed by sudden death. Cases should be referred to a veterinarian, who will recommend control measures to be taken.

Ringworm: In spite of its name, ringworm has nothing to do with worms, but is a fungus infection of the skin. Symptoms appear as small, bald patches containing circular raised patches of skin, yellowish or grayish in color. Normally starting in the head or face region, if left untreated, ringworm will spread to other parts of the body, causing loss of coat and condition. A daily application of tincture of iodine to the infected areas will normally effect a cure in a few days.

Snuffles: Modern methods of husbandry have made this disease scarce; at one time it was the scourge of the rabbitry and the loss of many animals could be attributed to it. Snuffles appears as a heavy yellow discharge from the nose, which the rabbit will continually attempt to wipe with its front paws. Constant coughing, sneezing and labored breathing will also be apparent and the animal suffers much distress. In itself, snuffles is not generally fatal, but complications such as pneumonia often follow, resulting in death. It is best to destroy rabbits suffering from chronic snuffles although there is evidence that certain modern antibiotics will effect a cure. Provided rabbits are kept in dry, well ventilated but draft free conditions, and receive a balanced diet, it is most unlikely that this disease will gain a foothold.

Right: *Handling feral rabbits is not advised.*

Tuberculosis: Now fortunately, very rare in domestic rabbits, it was at one time quite common in stock which was fed habitually on infected cows milk.

Vent Disease: This is a form of venereal disease caused by an organism known as a spirochete and is passed from one animal to the next during mating. Symptoms include inflammation of the

Above: Health is of primary concern to a commercial rabbit breeder, especially if rabbits are raised for the laboratory.

genitals, manifesting itself in large sores which may spread to the anus and eventually to the mouth and face. Fortunately, this disease responds well to antibiotic injections administered by a vet.

Right: A young Netherland Dwarf rabbit showing no signs of disease. Photo by Michael Gilroy.

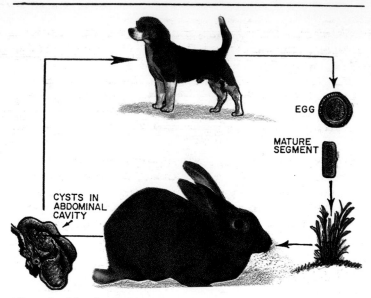

Life cycle of the dog tape worm.

Worm Infections: There are various types of internal parasitic worms which may infect rabbits, including tapeworms and roundworms. These are transmitted from the droppings of an infected animal via the food, so strict hygiene is the major preventive measure.

Animals with heavy worm infestations may become anemic and lose condition. There are various excellent proprietary worming compounds available, and these should be administered according to the manufacturer's instructions.

Breeding

To most rabbit fanciers, the most exciting part of their hobby is the breeding of new stock. There is nothing to describe the excitement and interest generated each time a doe in kindle approaches the point of giving birth. Rabbits are prolific breeders and it is by no means difficult to get them to have young; the hard part lies in producing good show specimens.

Sexing

Obviously, if one wishes to breed rabbits, it is necessary to have a true pair, a buck, or male rabbit and a doe, or female. It is fairly easy to sex adult rabbits; the male will have a prominent scrotum which is obviously not apparent on the female. As the scrotum takes some time to develop, the sexing of young rabbits is not quite so simple. It is best for two people to examine rabbits for sexing, one holding the rabbit while the other manipulates the genitalia. The rabbit is held belly upwards, preferably laid on a flat surface for stability and the hind legs are spread apart. Using the forefinger and thumb, the other person applies gentle pressure to either side of the vent until either the penis of the buck or the vaginal opening of the doe is seen. The distance from the sex organ to the anus is about twice as much in the male as in the female.

Sexual Maturity

Sexual maturity is reached when the male is capable of producing sperm and passing them to the female during the mating process, and the female is capable of producing fertile ova. The age at which sexual maturity occurs varies from one breed to another, and sometimes is affected by the type of diet received by the growing young; those having a poor diet will obviously take longer to mature. In general, the smaller the breed the sooner the animals will reach sexual maturity. Netherland Dwarfs, for instance, can be sexually mature as early as three months, while a Flemish Giant may be as old as eight months before it is capable of reproducing.

Selection and Mating

The selection of suitable pairs for mating is of particular importance if one intends to breed good exhibition specimens. Obviously one will have already decided what breed, if any, one wishes to procreate and it will be necessary to mate together the best possible specimens of the chosen type. It is best to obtain the original pair from a successful breeder of that variety. Admittedly, you will not get his best stock; he will want that himself for future breeding, but it should be possible to obtain specimens of a

Sexing a male rabbit. When the abdomen is pressed, the penis will protrude.

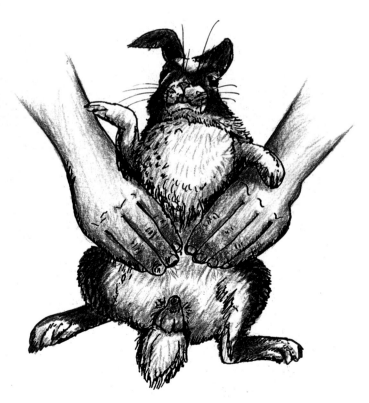

standard suitable for starting a new line. In order to produce the best quality youngsters, the breeder selects the most outstanding buck and doe available and mates them together, in the hope that the resulting youngsters will possess the best features of both parents. This sounds easy but often it does not quite work out; there is always an element

The inheritance of coat color in rabbits is not a simple subject, and breeding for color in rabbits demands study and planning.

of chance when breeding rabbits, which undoubtedly adds to the excitement of the hobby. After several years of experience and several generations of rabbits, the novice breeder will soon learn which animals are most likely to pass their outstanding qualities on to their offspring, and which individuals are likely to produce inferior young, even if of good quality themselves.

It is wise to keep accurate and up-to-date records of all rabbit matings, starting at the very first one; it is amazing how quickly one can forget which was the sire or dam of a certain individual unless the animals are marked and the breeder is able to refer to a record

Below: *Genitalia of a female rabbit. Susceptible to venereal diseases, regular examination of the genitalia is useful. Photo by Bruce Crook.*

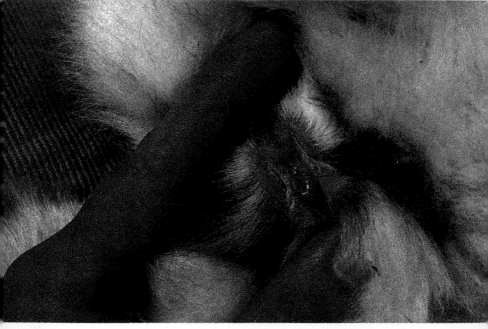

card. By keeping details of sire and dam, exhibition history, ailments and treatment and other relevant information, the breeder will soon build up an invaluable source of reference material both for him/herself and future fanciers.

Breeding pairs are kept separate until in prime condition before mating is attempted. If the pair is newly acquired, it is best to keep them apart for at least fourteen days, giving them a balanced diet and allowing them to become accustomed to their new quarters before

Above: *A uniform marking is the goal of breeders of the English rabbit. Photo by Michael Gilroy.*

introducing them. It is usual to take the doe to the buck's hutch for mating, as he is more likely to perform successfully on his own territory. In mature adults there should be no problem in achieving a quick mating response; unlike many other groups of mammals, lagomorphs do not have specific periods of estrus when conception is possible. The female rabbit is stimulated into immediate ovulation by the courtship activities

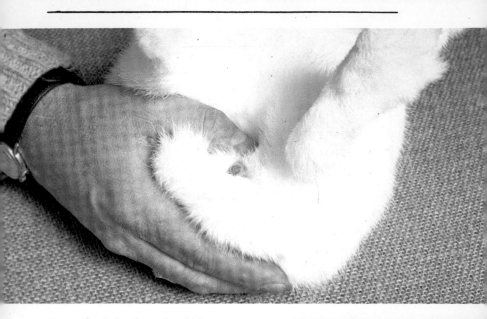

Above: *Genitalia of a male rabbit. The genital area is sensitive, so medications should be applied with care. Photo by Vince Serbin.*

of the male and allows copulation to take place. This may happen at any time of the year but is most likely to be successful in spring, summer or autumn. The act of copulation in rabbits is extremely fast, and the person who witnesses it for the first time finds it hard to believe that such a brief encounter can lead to a successful pregnancy. So do not be unduly worried if your buck mounts the doe and literally falls off exhausted after only a few seconds.

Pregnancy
The doe is returned to the maternity hutch as soon as

mating is accomplished. At this time it is wise to see that she has all the necessary refinements to make her period of pregnancy comfortable; a description of a breeding hutch, with its nest compartment, and rest platform for the doe has been described in the first chapter. Where there is no separate nesting compartment in the hutch, the doe must be supplied with a nesting box, similar to that described for the sleeping box. Adequate nesting material should be provided and the pregnant doe will soon busy herself preparing a nest for the birth of her litter.

Sometimes a doe may build her nest outside the compartment or nest box, in which case the nest should be moved back into the compartment. This may be repeated two or three

Below: *A pair of Himalayan rabbits mating. It is normal practice to remove the buck after mating. Photo by Michael Gilroy.*

times, but if the rabbit persists in having her nest where *she* wants it, it is best to leave it in position and cover part of the hutch front with sacking, rather than disturb her too much and risk losing the litter.

The rabbit's average gestation period is thirty one days, although this may occasionally vary as much as five days in either direction. It is not always easy to ascertain whether a doe is pregnant or *in kindle,* as fanciers are apt to say, until the later stages of the pregnancy.

Above: *The Dutch marking is available in many color combinations besides black. Photo by Michael Gilroy.*

One method which is sometimes used is to reintroduce the doe to the buck about two days after the original mating. If she is already pregnant she will supposedly repel the amorous advances of the male in no uncertain manner; however, this method is certainly not foolproof and it has been proven that certain does will allow further copulation, even when in kindle.

Later in the pregnancy, a doe will increase in girth and it will be possible to feel the young through the abdomen walls by palpation. Pregnant does should always be handled as little and as gently as possible though and when feeling for young, this should be done with the fingertips applying the minimum amount of pressure. Towards the end of the pregnancy, when the birth of the litter is imminent, it is best to cease handling the doe altogether, but to ensure that she has adequate nest material. She will begin to line the nest with fur plucked from her own belly and make a really cozy nursery.

Sometimes a pregnant doe will lose her appetite shortly before the birth of her litter and she may void soft droppings. These are perfectly natural occurrences and are no cause for concern; after the birth she will speedily

Below: *The blaze is the white part on the face, as seen in this Chocolate Dutch rabbit. Photo by Michael Gilroy.*

return to her normal feeding pattern. A pregnant doe is always more thirsty than usual so the water supply should be checked at least twice a day during this period; does which are thirsty when they give birth are likely to devour their own babies, so precaution is necessary. During the pregnancy, the doe should be given a slight increase in green food and fresh vegetables but at the same time, do not overdo it, the dangers of which have already been described.

Above: *A litter of Lops. Eyes are already open and they are now eager to move about. Photo by Bruce Crook.*

Some breeders like to give their pregnant does a little diluted cow's milk each day (two parts milk and one part water) and this can be continued right through to just before the weaning of the litter. There is certainly no harm in this and the dangers of tuberculosis in the milk are long past. As milk sours very quickly, it should not be left in the hutch for long periods.

Rearing

The doe should be left completely undisturbed when the birth is imminent; many litters have been lost due to the impatience of the breeder. After birth, the doe will obviously appear slimmer and slight movements in the nesting material will indicate that all is well. Allow about twenty-four hours after the birth before inspecting the litter. Remove the doe gently from the hutch and give her something to eat to occupy her while this is being done. Before touching the young, it is advisable to rub the hands in some of the floor litter, thus minimizing the risk of the human scent being left on the babies which might upset the doe.

Baby rabbits (sometimes called kittens) are born almost devoid of fur, are totally blind, as their eyelids are still fused, and the ears are rather short. In fact, on seeing a litter of newborn rabbits for the first time, many people find it hard to believe that they are not rats or guinea pigs! In marked breeds, it is already possible to see the skin pigmentation at this

Below: *The fuzzy material in the nest is fur pulled by the doe from her own chest to keep the babies warm.*

stage, giving some indication as to how good they are going to be. Any dead babies, which occasionally occur in a litter, should be removed and disposed of. At this time any obvious runts should be destroyed and a decision made as to whether any are to be fostered to another doe. The size of a litter can vary

Above: *Baby rabbits stay close together for warmth. Be sure the nest is free from draft; rabbits catch colds easily.*

from one to as many as fifteen youngsters and sometimes it is best to remove part of a large litter, to be reared by a doe with a small litter. For this reason, it is advisable to pair up several does at the same time, so that large and small litters can be evened out by fostering. The safest time to remove young for fostering to another doe is when they are about three days old, although sometimes they can be left up to ten days. In general, the older the young are, the less chance there is of a fostering being successful. It is wise to remove the doe from the hutch when removing young, as well as removing the foster mother before placing them in her nest. In this way, neither parent should be unduly worried to find a few less or a few more young when they are returned. Usually the best number of young for a doe to comfortably rear is about six, and some breeders will limit themselves to this number per litter, even if it means culling off some of the young.

Once the young have been sorted out, the mother rabbits should be left in peace to rear their babies. In most cases

Below: *Nest with Siamese Satins. The shadings on the ears are already evident.*

there should be no problems until weaning time approaches. At about ten days old, the youngsters' eyes will open and they will soon leave the nest for periods and explore the hutch. The doe will make an excellent parent and do all she can to keep her youngsters in good health. She will regulate the temperature of the nest by removing or adding nest materials as necessary, so it is advisable to ensure that a little extra bedding is always available. She will allow her youngsters to suckle as often as is necessary and they will know by instinct how to feed. She will keep the nest clean, and remove soiled material, replacing it with fresh.

At three weeks of age, the young rabbits will be leaving the nest regularly, and this is the safest time to give them their first thorough inspection, and check for any abnormalities. At this age, young rabbits are susceptible to minor eye infections and, if any weeping is observed, the eyes should be bathed with a little boracic solution and treated with a good veterinary eye ointment. Particular attention should

be paid to hutch cleanliness at this time as young rabbits will not yet have acquired their full immunity to infectious diseases and of course, with a mother and growing

Above: *With passage of time, bond between doe and litter weakens, and she may be ready to breed again.*

litter in the hutch, the bedding will become soiled more frequently than usual. At this time the young will begin to try solid food and it is essential that this be clean, wholesome and given frequently, the quantity increased as the rabbits grow. Sudden changes in the diet should be strictly avoided, as the

delicate stomachs of the young will be unable to withstand such practices.

Weaning
Weaning is the process of ceasing to take the mother's milk and proceeding onto a normal adult diet. The doe's milk supply normally begins to dry up at about six weeks after the birth and will have totally ceased by the eighth week. During this time, the youngsters will be taking less and less milk (indeed the doe will start discouraging them), and eating more solid food. At weaning time, a close watch should be kept on the doe as this is the time she may turn nasty towards her young. In the wild of course, she would drive them out of her burrow so that they are forced to start fending for themselves, but this would be somewhat difficult when confined to a hutch. Preferably the doe should be removed from the litter and placed in a hutch on her own; the young can be left in the nursery hutch for a few more days until they get over the trauma of losing their mother. They may then be placed into stock hutches or Morant pens, does separated from the bucks. If the young are to be sold, now is the best time to do it; but obviously retaining the best specimens for one's own future breeding!

The doe should now be thoroughly examined to see that she has come unscathed through the

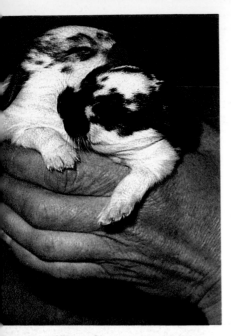

Above: *Close-up view of eight-day-old Lops. Note the large ears, naturally folded down.* Photo by Bruce Crook.

or eleven litters a year, but in each case the litter is fostered to another rabbit. This is not so bad as the doe is spared the most exhausting task of rearing the young.

Pseudo Pregnancy
Occasionally, a doe which has apparently been successfully mated will go through all the outward signs of being pregnant, even down to increasing in weight and building a nest. No litter arrives, however, and the breeder becomes somewhat disconcerted. What will have happened is that the mating will have been sterile for some reason or another. Usually the doe may be successfully mated the second time around.

Period of Fertility
The average length of life of a domestic rabbit is about five years, but there are records of some specimens living for twelve years or more. The period of highest fertility for a doe is usually about three years, say from the ages of one to four, though even this will vary from breed to breed. In general, it is safe to say that a doe should not be bred before it is nine months old, nor after it has completed its fourth

process of pregnancy and rearing the litter. Some breeders like to mate the doe almost immediately and let her have three or four litters in succession through the warmer months; others may allow the doe to rest for two or three weeks between litters. As long as the doe appears to be in top condition, there is no reason why she cannot have three or four litters in succession, but for the average doe this should be the maximum per year. Some breeders allow a good doe to have up to ten season. Litters born outside of these guidelines are more likely to be inferior in quantity, quality and weight. Bucks on the other hand may be used for stud purposes at any time from sexual maturity, almost to the end of their lives. A good buck is capable of mating almost daily if allowed to, though this is not strictly necessary, and it is most unlikely that any fancier would have sufficient does to experiment. However, it will not do a buck any harm to put him to a doe about once per week provided he receives a balanced diet. Outside the mating sessions, the stud bucks should be kept well away from the does, but when introduced to each other, mating should take place in a very short time.

Below: *These well marked Checkered Giants will mature into large rabbits, the self-colored ones (Netherland Dwarf) will be small. Photo by Michael Gilroy.*

Hand Rearing

On occasion, it may be necessary to hand rear a litter. This would be in the case of the death or severe illness of the mother or, in the event of mastitis, her refusal to feed the litter due to pain.

If there is no available foster mother, the only way to save the litter will be to hand rear it. This is a time consuming task and one which requires a great deal of patience, but if successful, gives one a wonderful feeling of accomplishment. Another advantage of hand rearing is that the youngsters will make excellent pet rabbits, losing all fear of their human foster parents. As rabbit milk is one of the most highly concentrated of all domestic animals, it is necessary to make a good, strong mix for the youngsters. A good quality powdered baby milk should be used and mixed to a concentration one and a half times as strong as that recommended for human babies. The milk should be made lukewarm and fed to the baby rabbits from an eye dropper, a pipette or a doll's feeding bottle. The amount taken will be ascertained by trial and error, and initially, the youngsters should be fed about every three hours. After a week this can be reduced to every four hours and so on until they are three weeks of age. At this stage they should be encouraged to take some solid food and the milk can be further reduced until they are seven weeks old and can be weaned off it altogether.

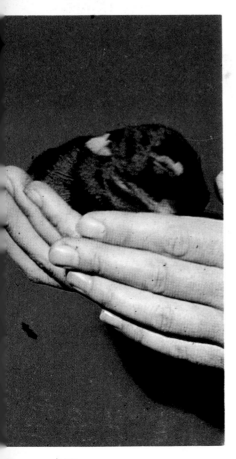

Below: *An 11-day-old Tan. Tan marking is visible as soon as the fur develops. Photo by Ray Hanson.*

Exhibition

Keepers and breeders of all kinds of domestic animals at some time get the urge to show off their stock to others and the beginnings start with the child who proudly shows his or her first pet rabbit to Auntie. Later on the more serious fancier will want to show his animals to friends and neighbors. Unfortunately, unless the spectators are rabbit fanciers themselves, the interest shown will be only cursory. The answer is to join a club and mingle with people who have similar interests; it is only then that one will begin to get the full benefit and excitement from one's chosen hobby. There are rabbit clubs in most major populated areas in most countries and it is usually fairly easy to find out where they are. Your pet shop proprietor will be able to inform you; you may get the information from the local library, the newspaper, from another breeder or through a specialist periodical.

Above: *Rabbits can easily be trained to take food from your fingers—but don't spoil them!*

The smaller clubs are usually affiliated with larger clubs, which again may be members of a National Federation. There are clubs for general rabbit keepers, and other clubs for particular breeds. In the United Kingdom the British Rabbit Council is the body which lays down the rules for exhibiting and awards diplomas for prize winning stock. Each club has regular shows; there are local club shows, regional shows and national shows. If a show is classified as an open show, it means anyone may enter; if it is a club show it means that only members of the club may enter. Most of the larger clubs publish their own newsletters which inform members of the results of shows, as well as giving useful information on general husbandry, nutrition, new breeds, chit chat and various other items of interest to the rabbit enthusiast. Regular attendance at meetings will give one a chance to discuss one's interests with other fanciers, examine the competition and gain the benefit of the experience of the veterans in the hobby.

Preparing for a Show

The keeping, breeding and ultimate showing of rabbits nearly always follows a natural progression.

Below: *First step in judging a rabbit is to check the identification. Photo by Mervin F. Roberts.*

Starting with a single pet rabbit, the novice will first get to know the individual animal and later on, will decide to make an attempt at breeding. This may be done by obtaining a mate for one's original pet, or by purchasing a pair of a particular breed. After one or two litters of pet rabbits have been produced, the fancier will already begin to get a feel for the hobby and, of course, all the time will be building up valuable experience. While this is going on it is very useful to be a member of a club, to regularly attend meetings and, in particular, shows where one can inspect the

Above: In addition to ribbons, trophies or other items are awarded to the winners. Photo by Vince Serbin.

winners and the losers and take notes of the points which make prizewinners.

Having decided on the breed, and begun to produce litters, it may be a while before one decides that one has a good show specimen. Rabbit showing is an art which cannot be learned overnight and the successful exhibitor will have first spent many hours working with and handling his rabbits and studying the factors which are most likely to result in a good pairing.

Preparing for a Show

Once a potential show specimen has been produced, the most important single factor in bringing it into prime condition is good husbandry. The animal should be kept in a clean, draft-proof hutch, given a good balanced diet and handled regularly. The handling of show rabbits is very important; it would be a mistake to think that a nervous, flighty animal would give a favorable impression on the show bench. The rabbit should be groomed daily, preferably at the same time. It may be placed on a table or other clean flat surface and gently brushed to remove loose hair and help to bring the coat into fine condition. The coat of a healthy rabbit should show a fine gloss or bloom, and this is one of the first things a judge will look for. A good finish can be applied to the coat by rubbing a silky cloth over it.

Below: *A three-week-old blue Silver Fox rabbit asleep on slab of stone. Photo by Michael Gilroy.*

A rabbit which is molting should never be entered in a show. This will only result in the animal losing valuable points. Animals which are sick, ailing or even slightly out of condition obviously should not be entered; apart from the risk of disease being introduced into other exhibitors stock, the penalty for such an indiscretion can be severe. Light colored rabbits occasionally show stains on the coat, particularly on the feet and underside.

Above: *A satin fur certainly enhances the appearance of this Tan rabbit. Photo by Michael Gilroy.*

These can be removed by a gentle sponging over with warm water and soap or shampoo (not detergent), just before the show. Never try to cheat by using powder or dye on the coat to 'improve' the color; such things will not be overlooked by the experienced judge and will only lead to disqualification.

Transport

When transporting animals to a show, or elsewhere, it is wise to have proper travelling boxes. These will ensure the comfort of the animals on prolonged trips. A travelling box is made from lightweight material, such as plywood, and may be purchased or constructed at home by the handyman. The size will vary, depending on the breed to be exhibited, but a box for a medium sized breed, such as Dutch or English, can be 35 cm (14 in) long, by 25 cm (10 in) wide, by 30 cm (12 in) high. Adequate ventilation holes should be drilled in the upper part of the ends and also in the lid. The size of the holes should be large enough to allow a good flow of air, but small enough to stop curious people from poking at the animals while they are in transit. The boxes may be varnished or painted with a good quality lead-free paint. Never transport more than one rabbit in a travelling box unless it is divided into compartments; otherwise the animals may fight, or soil each other's coats. The floor of the box should be layered with clean wood shavings and a little hay should be given

Below: *A portable cage should have secure handles. Photo by Vince Serbin.*

Above: *Carrying cages can be lashed together and towed as a unit. Photo by Bruce Crook.*

for the animals to nibble at in transit. Never give water, green food or vegetables to animals going to a show as this may result in staining of the coat; they will receive adequate provisions when they arrive.

At the Show

On arrival at the show the animals will be allocated a number and a pen, where they will stay until the time of judging. They can be given a final polish with a silk cloth and the owner will then retire until the judging is over. Stewards are normally responsible for taking the animals out of the pens for the judge to inspect. To keep things fair, the judge will be unaware of the rabbit's owner and will know the animal by number only.

There may be several kinds of classes or schedules at a show, ranging from pet classes, where the animals are judged on health and condition alone, to specialist classes for the different breeds, in which case the animals are judged on the standards laid down by the appropriate body. These may include quality of fur, weight, shape, and markings. Sometimes there is a special prize for the animal which is 'best in show', a very prestigious honor to accomplish. Beginners are advised not to be too ambitious to start with and should confine themselves to the pet classes in order to gain experience. Never be too disappointed if your first exhibit is not a winner; even this counts towards experience and you will almost certainly have better luck next time around.

Index

A Himalayan marked Netherland Dwarf rabbit. Photo by Michael Gilroy.

Front cover photo by Burkhard Kahl of European domesticated rabbits. Upper back cover photo of Dutch rabbits; lower photo by Texas Agricultural Extension Service of white Polish rabbit.

Easy to read and loaded with practical, easy-to-apply information and solidly sensible advice, this highly colorful book covers every topic of importance to anyone—especially a beginner—interested in keeping rabbits. Vital information is provided about the different types of rabbits and what they need in order to live well: how to house and feed them, how to breed them, how to keep them healthy.

ISBN 0-86622-281-2

9 780866 222815